TEACHER'S PET PUBLICATIONS

LITPLAN TEACHER PACK
for
Hamlet
based on the book by
William Shakespeare

Written by
Mary B. Collins

© 1997 Teacher's Pet Publications
All Rights Reserved

This **LitPlan** for William Shakespeare's
Hamlet
has been brought to you by Teacher's Pet Publications, Inc.

Copyright Teacher's Pet Publications 1997
11504 Hammock Point
Berlin MD 21811

Only the student materials in this unit plan
(such as worksheets, study questions, assignment sheets, and tests)
may be reproduced multiple times for use in the purchaser's classroom.

For any additional copyright questions,
contact Teacher's Pet Publications.

www.tpet.com

TABLE OF CONTENTS - *Hamlet*

Introduction	10
Unit Objectives	13
Reading Assignment Sheet	14
Unit Outline	15
Study Questions (Short Answer)	19
Quiz/Study Questions (Multiple Choice)	26
Pre-reading Vocabulary Worksheets	43
Lesson One (Introductory Lesson)	51
Nonfiction Assignment Sheet	54
Oral Reading Evaluation Form	58
Writing Assignment 1	60
Writing Assignment 2	66
Writing Assignment 3	76
Writing Evaluation Form	67
Vocabulary Review Activities	65
Extra Writing Assignments/Discussion ?s	70
Unit Review Activities	78
Unit Tests	81
Unit Resource Materials	121
Vocabulary Resource Materials	137

ABOUT THE AUTHOR
William Shakespeare

SHAKESPEARE, William (1564-1616). For more than 350 years, William Shakespeare has been the world's most popular playwright. On the stage, in the movies, and on television his plays are watched by vast audiences. People read his plays again and again for pleasure. Students reading his plays for the first time are delighted by what they find.

Shakespeare's continued popularity is due to many things. His plays are filled with action, his characters are believable, and his language is thrilling to hear or read. Underlying all this is Shakespeare's deep humanity. He was a profound student of people and he understood them. He had a great tolerance, sympathy, and love for all people, good or evil.

While watching a Shakespearean tragedy, the audience is moved and shaken. After the show the spectators are calm, washed clean of pity and terror. They are saddened but at peace, repeating the old saying, "There, but for the grace of God, go I."

A Shakespearean comedy is full of fun. The characters are lively; the dialogue is witty. In the end young lovers are wed; old babblers are silenced; wise men are content. The comedies are joyous and romantic.

Boyhood in Stratford

William Shakespeare was born in Stratford-upon-Avon, England, in 1564. This was the sixth year of the reign of Queen Elizabeth I. He was christened on April 26 of that year. The day of his birth is unknown. It has long been celebrated on April 23, the feast of St. George.

He was the third child and oldest son of John and Mary Arden Shakespeare. Two sisters, Joan and Margaret, died before he was born. The other children were Gilbert, a second Joan, Anne, Richard, and Edmund. Only the second Joan outlived William.

Shakespeare's father was a tanner and glovemaker. He was an alderman of Stratford for years. He also served a term as high bailiff, or mayor. Toward the end of his life John Shakespeare lost most of his money. When he died in 1601, he left William only a little real estate. Not much is known about Mary Shakespeare, except that she came from a wealthier family than her husband.

Stratford-upon-Avon is in Warwickshire, called the heart of England. In Shakespeare's day it was well farmed and heavily wooded. The town itself was prosperous and progressive.

The town was proud of its grammar school. Young Shakespeare went to it, although when or for how long is not known. He may have been a pupil there between his 7th and 13th years. His studies must have been mainly in Latin. The schooling was good. All four schoolmasters at the school during Shakespeare's boyhood were graduates of Oxford University.

Nothing definite is known about his boyhood. From the content of his plays, he must have learned early about the woods and fields, about birds, insects, and small animals, about trades and outdoor sports, and about the country people he later portrayed with such good humor. Then and later he picked up an amazing stock of facts about hunting, hawking, fishing, dances, music, and other arts and sports. Among other subjects, he also learned about alchemy, astrology, folklore, medicine, and law. As good writers do, he collected information both from books and from daily observation of the world around him.

Marriage and Life in London

In 1582, when he was 18, he married Anne Hathaway. She was from Shottery, a village a mile from Stratford. Anne was seven or eight years older than Shakespeare. From this difference in their ages, a story arose that they were unhappy together. Their first daughter, Susanna, was born in 1583. In 1585 a twin boy and girl, Hamnet and Judith, were born.

What Shakespeare did between 1583 and 1592 is not known. Various stories are told. He may have taught school, worked in a lawyer's office, served on a rich man's estate, or traveled with a company of actors. One famous story says that about 1584 he and some friends were caught poaching on the estate of Sir Thomas Lucy of Carlecote, near Warwick, and were forced to leave town. A less likely story is that he was in London in 1588. There he was supposed to have held horses for theater patrons and later to have worked in the theaters as a callboy.

By 1592, however, Shakespeare was definitely in London and was already recognized as an actor and playwright. He was then 28 years old. In that year he was referred to in another man's book for the first time. Robert Greene, a playwright, accused him of borrowing from the plays of others.

Between 1592 and 1594, plague kept the London theaters closed most of the time. During these years Shakespeare wrote his earliest sonnets and two long narrative poems, 'Venus and Adonis' and 'The Rape of Lucrece'. Both were printed by Richard Field, a boyhood friend from Stratford. They were well received and helped establish him as a poet.

Shakespeare Prospers

Until 1598 Shakespeare's theater work was confined to a district northeast of London. This was outside the walls, in the parish of Shoreditch. Located there were two playhouses, the Theatre and the Curtain. Both were managed by James Burbage, whose son Richard Burbage was Shakespeare's friend and the greatest tragic actor of his day.

Up to 1596 Shakespeare lived near these theaters in Bishopsgate, where the North Road entered the city. Sometime between 1596 and 1599, he moved across the Thames River to a district called Bankside. There, two theaters, the Rose and the Swan, had been built by Philip Henslowe. He was James Burbage's chief competitor in London as a theater manager.

The Burbages also moved to this district in 1598 and built the famous Globe Theatre. Its sign showed Atlas supporting the world-hence the theater's name. Shakespeare was associated with the Globe Theatre for the rest of his active life. He owned shares in it, which brought him much money.

Meanwhile, in 1597, Shakespeare had bought New Place, the largest house in Stratford. During the next three years he bought other property in Stratford and in London. The year before, his father, probably at Shakespeare's suggestion, applied for and was granted a coat of arms. It bore the motto Non sanz droict-Not without right. From this time on, Shakespeare could write "Gentleman" after his name. This meant much to him, for in his day actors were classed legally with criminals and vagrants.

Shakespeare's name first appeared on the title pages of his printed plays in 1598. In the same year Francis Meres, in 'Palladis Tamia: Wit's Treasury', praised him as a poet and dramatist. Meres's comments on 12 of Shakespeare's plays showed that Shakespeare's genius was recognized in his own time.

Honored As Actor and Playwright

Queen Elizabeth I died in 1603. King James I followed her to the throne. Shakespeare's theatrical company was taken under the king's patronage and called the King's Company. Shakespeare and the other actors were made officers of the royal household. The theatrical company was the most successful of its time. Before it was the King's Company, it had been known as the Earl of Derby's and the Lord Chamberlain's. In 1608 the company acquired the Blackfriars Theatre. This was a smaller and more aristocratic theater than the Globe. Thereafter the company alternated between the two playhouses.

Plays by Shakespeare were performed at both theaters, at the royal court, and in the castles of the nobles. After 1603 Shakespeare probably acted little, although he was still a good actor. His favorite roles seem to have been old Adam in 'As You Like It' and the Ghost in 'Hamlet'.

In 1607, when he was 43, he may have suffered a serious physical breakdown. In the same year his older daughter Susanna married John Hall, a doctor. The next year Shakespeare's first grandchild, Elizabeth, was born. Also in 1607 his brother Edmund, who had been an actor in London, died at the age of 27.

The Mermaid Tavern Group

About this time Shakespeare became one of the group of now-famous writers who gathered at the Mermaid Tavern in Cheapside. The club was formed by Sir Walter Raleigh. Ben Jonson was its leading spirit (see Jonson). Shakespeare was a popular member. He was admired for his talent and loved for his kindliness. Thomas Fuller, writing about 50 years later, gave an amusing account of the conversational duels between Shakespeare and Jonson:

"Many were the wit-combats betwixt him and Ben Jonson; which two I behold like a Spanish great galleon and an English man-of-war; Master Jonson (like the former) was built far higher in learning; solid, but slow, in his performances. Shakespeare, with the English man-of-war, lesser in bulk, but lighter in sailing, could turn with all tides, tack about, and take advantage of all winds, by the quickness of his wit and invention."

Jonson sometimes criticized Shakespeare harshly. Nevertheless he later wrote a eulogy of Shakespeare that is remarkable for its feeling and acuteness. In it he said:

> Leave thee alone, for the comparison
> Of all that insolent Greece or haughty Rome
> Sent forth, or since did from their ashes come.
> Triumph, my Britain, thou hast one to show
> To whom all scenes of Europe homage owe.
> He was not of an age, but for all time!
> . . . .
> Sweet Swan of Avon! what a sight it were
> To see thee in our waters yet appear,
> And make those flights upon the banks of Thames,
> That so did take Eliza, and our James!

Death and Burial at Stratford

Shakespeare retired from his theater work in 1610 and returned to Stratford. His friends from London visited him. In 1613 the Globe Theatre burned. He lost much money in it, but he was still wealthy. He shared in the building of the new Globe. A few months before the fire he bought as an investment a house in the fashionable Blackfriars district of London.

On April 23, 1616, Shakespeare died at the age of 52. This date is according to the Old Style, or Julian, calendar of his time. The New Style, or Gregorian, calendar date is May 3, 1616. He was buried in the chancel of the Church of the Holy Trinity in Stratford.

A stone slab-a reproduction of the original one, which it replaced in 1830-marks his grave. It bears an inscription, perhaps written by himself.

On the north wall of the chancel is his monument. It consists of a portrait bust enclosed in a stone frame. Below it is an inscription in Latin and English. This bust and the engraving by Martin Droeshout, prefixed to the First Folio edition of his plays (1623), are the only pictures of Shakespeare which can be accepted as showing his true likeness.

John Aubrey, an English antiquarian, wrote about Shakespeare 65 years after the poet's death. He evidently used information furnished by the son of one of Shakespeare's fellow actors. Aubrey described him as "a handsome, well-shaped man, very good company, and of a ready and pleasant smooth wit."

Shakespeare's will, still in existence, bequeathed most of his property to Susanna and her daughter. He left small mementoes to friends. He mentioned his wife only once, leaving her his "second best bed" with its furnishings.

Much has been written about this odd bequest. There is little reason to think it was a slight. Indeed, it may have been a special mark of affection. The "second best bed" was probably the one they used. The best bed was reserved for guests. At any rate, his wife was entitled by law to one third of her husband's goods and real estate and to the use of their home for life. She died in 1623.

The will contains three signatures of Shakespeare. These, with three others, are the only known specimens of his handwriting in existence. Several experts also regard some lines in the manuscript of 'Sir Thomas More' as Shakespeare's own handwriting. He spelled his name in
various ways. His father's papers show about 16 spellings. Shakspere, Shaxpere, and Shakespeare are the most common.

Did Shakespeare Really Write the Plays?

The outward events of Shakespeare's life are ordinary. He was hard-working, sober, and middle-class in his ways. He steadily gathered wealth and took good care of his family. Many people have found it impossible to believe that such a man could have written the plays. They feel that he could not have known such heights and depths of passion. They believe that the people around Shakespeare expressed little realization of his greatness. Some say that a man of his little schooling could not have learned about the professions, the aristocratic sports of hawking and hunting, the speech and manners of the upper classes.

Since the 1800's there has been a steady effort to prove that Shakespeare did not write the plays or that others did. For a long time the leading candidate was Sir Francis Bacon. Books on the Shakespeare-Bacon argument would fill a library (see Bacon, Francis). After Bacon became less popular, the Earl of Oxford and then other men were suggested as the authors. Nearly every famous

Elizabethan was named. The most recent has been Christopher Marlowe. Some people even claim that "Shakespeare" is an assumed name for a whole group of poets and playwrights.

However, some men around Shakespeare-for example, Meres in 1598 and Jonson in 1623-did recognize his worth as a man and as a writer. To argue that an obscure Stratford boy could not have become the Shakespeare of literature is to ignore the mystery of genius. His knowledge is of the kind that could not be learned in school. It is the kind that only a genius could learn, by applying a keen intelligence to everyday life. Some great writers have had even less schooling than Shakespeare.

Few scholars take seriously these attempts to deprive Shakespeare of credit. Shakespeare's style is individual and cannot be imitated. Any good student recognizes it. It can be found nowhere else. Bacon is a poor candidate for the honor. Great as he was, he was certainly not a poet.

How the Plays Came Down to Us

Since the 1700's scholars have worked over the text of Shakespeare's plays. They have had to do so because the plays were badly printed, and no original manuscripts of them survive.

In Shakespeare's day plays were not usually printed under the author's supervision. When a playwright sold a play to his company, he lost all rights to it. He could not sell it again to a publisher without the company's consent. When the play was no longer in demand on the stage, the company itself might sell the manuscript. Plays were eagerly read by the Elizabethan public. This was even more true during the plague years, when the theaters were closed. It was also true during times of business depression. Sometimes plays were taken down in shorthand and sold. At other times, a dismissed actor would write down the play from memory and sell it.

About half of Shakespeare's plays were printed during his lifetime in small, cheap pamphlets called quartos. Most of these were made from fairly accurate manuscripts. A few were in garbled form.

In 1623, seven years after Shakespeare's death, his collected plays were published in a large, expensive volume called the First Folio. It contains all his plays except two of which he wrote only part-'Pericles' and 'Two Noble Kinsmen'. It also has the first engraved portrait of Shakespeare.

This edition was authorized by Shakespeare's acting group, the King's Company. Some of the plays in it were printed from the accurate quartos and some from manuscripts in the theater. It is certain that many of these manuscripts were in Shakespeare's own handwriting. Others were copies. Still others, like the 'Hamlet' manuscript, had been revised by another dramatist.

Shakespearean scholars have been determining what Shakespeare actually wrote. They have done so by studying the language, stagecraft, handwriting, and printing of the period and by carefully examining and comparing the different editions. They have modernized spelling and punctuation, supplied stage directions, explained difficult passages, and made the plays easier for the modern reader to understand.

Another hard task has been to find out when the plays were written. About half of them have no definite date of composition. The plays themselves have been searched for clues. Other books have been examined. Scholars have tried to match events in Shakespeare's life with the subject matter of his plays.

These scholars have used detective methods. They have worked with clues, deduction, shrewd reasoning, and external and internal evidence. External evidence consists of actual references in other books. Internal evidence is made up of verse tests and a study of the poet's imagery and figures of speech, which changed from year to year.

The verse tests follow the idea that a poet becomes more skillful with practice. Scholars long ago noticed that in his early plays Shakespeare used little prose, much rhyme, and certain types of rhythmical and metrical regularity. As he grew older he used more prose, less rhyme, and greater freedom and variety in rhythm and meter. From these facts, scholars have figured out the dates of those plays that had none.

Shakespeare As a Dramatist

The facts about Shakespeare are interesting in themselves, but they have little to do with his place in literature. Shakespeare wrote his plays to give pleasure. It is possible to spoil that pleasure by giving too much attention to his life, his times, and the problem of figuring out what he actually wrote. He can be enjoyed in book form, in the theater, or on television without our knowing any of these things.

Some difficulties stand in the way of this enjoyment. Shakespeare wrote more than 350 years ago. The language he used is naturally somewhat different from the language of today. Besides, he wrote in verse. Verse permits a free use of words that may not be understood by some readers. His plays are often fanciful. This may not appeal to matter-of-fact people who are used to modern realism. For all these reasons, readers may find him difficult. The worst handicap to enjoyment is the notion that Shakespeare is a "classic," a writer to be approached with awe.

The way to escape this last difficulty is to remember that Shakespeare wrote his plays for everyday people and that many in the audience were uneducated. They looked upon him as a funny, exciting, and lovable entertainer, not as a great poet. People today should read him as the people in his day listened to him. The excitement and enjoyment of the plays will banish most of the difficulties.

--- Courtesy of Compton's Learning Company

INTRODUCTION

This unit has been designed to develop students' reading, writing, thinking, and language skills through exercises and activities related to *Hamlet* by William Shakespeare. It includes twenty-four lessons, supported by extra resource materials.

The **introductory lesson** introduces students to Shakespeare and his times through a group research project. Following the introductory activity, students are given a transition to explain how the activity relates to the play they are about to read. Following the transition, students are given the materials they will be using during the unit. At the end of the lesson, students begin the pre-reading work for the first reading assignment.

The **reading assignments** are approximately thirty pages each; some are a little shorter while others are a little longer. Students have approximately 15 minutes of pre-reading work to do prior to each reading assignment. This pre-reading work involves reviewing the study questions for the assignment and doing some vocabulary work for some challenging vocabulary words they will encounter in their reading.

The **study guide questions** are fact-based questions; students can find the answers to these questions right in the text. These questions come in two formats: short answer or multiple choice. The best use of these materials is probably to use the short answer version of the questions as study guides for students (since answers will be more complete), and to use the multiple choice version for occasional quizzes. If your school has the appropriate equipment, it might be a good idea to make transparencies of your answer keys for the overhead projector.

The **vocabulary work** is intended to enrich students' vocabularies as well as to aid in the students' understanding of the play. Prior to each reading assignment, students will complete a two-part worksheet for approximately 10 vocabulary words in the upcoming reading assignment. Part I focuses on students' use of general knowledge and contextual clues by giving the sentence in which the word appears in the text. Students are then to write down what they think the words mean based on the words' usage. Part II nails down the definitions of the words by giving students dictionary definitions of the words and having students match the words to the correct definitions based on the words' contextual usage. Students should then have a thorough understanding of the words when they meet them in the text.

After each reading assignment, students will go back and formulate answers for the study guide questions. Discussion of these questions serves as a **review** of the most important events and ideas presented in the reading assignments.

After students complete reading the work, there is a **vocabulary review** lesson which pulls together all of the fragmented vocabulary lists for the reading assignments and gives students a review of all of the words they have studied.

Following the vocabulary review, a lesson is devoted to the **extra discussion questions/writing assignments**. These questions focus on interpretation, critical analysis and personal response, employing a variety of thinking skills and adding to the students' understanding of the play.

The **project** which follows the discussion questions deals with people who have been assassinated throughout history and focuses on how the assassinations affected the people of the country/world.

There are three **writing assignments** in this unit, each with the purpose of informing, persuading, or having students express personal opinions. The first assignment is to inform: students take the information they have gathered through research, group work and class discussion and organize it into a composition. The second assignment is to persuade: students pretend they are an advertising agency hired by a time travel company to make a brochure enticing people to join their tour which features, among other things, going to London in 1601 to see a production of Shakespeare's *Hamlet*. The third assignment is to give students the opportunity to express their own opinions: students tell what they would do in Hamlet's situation.

In addition, there is a **nonfiction reading assignment**. Students are required to read a piece of nonfiction related in some way to *Hamlet*. After reading their nonfiction pieces, students will fill out a worksheet on which they answer questions regarding facts, interpretation, criticism, and personal opinions. During one class period, students make **oral presentations** about the nonfiction pieces they have read. This not only exposes all students to a wealth of information, it also gives students the opportunity to practice **public speaking**. This nonfiction assignment is done in conjunction with the introductory research assignment.

The **review lesson** pulls together all of the aspects of the unit. The teacher is given four or five choices of activities or games to use which all serve the same basic function of reviewing all of the information presented in the unit.

The **unit test** comes in two formats: all multiple choice-matching-true/false or with a mixture of matching, short answer, multiple choice, and composition. As a convenience, two different tests for each format have been included. There is also an advanced short answer version of the unit test.

There are additional **support materials** included with this unit. The **extra activities section** includes suggestions for an in-class library, crossword and word search puzzles related to the play, and extra vocabulary worksheets. There is a list of **bulletin board ideas** which gives the teacher suggestions for bulletin boards to go along with this unit. In addition, there is a list of **extra class activities** the teacher could choose from to enhance the unit or as a substitution for an exercise the teacher might feel is inappropriate for his/her class. **Answer keys** are located directly after the **reproducible student materials** throughout the unit. The student materials may be reproduced for use in the teacher's classroom without infringement of copyrights. No other portion of this unit may be reproduced without the written consent of Teacher's Pet Publications, Inc.

The **level** of this unit can be varied depending upon the criteria on which the individual assignments are graded, the teacher's expectations of his/her students in class discussions, and the formats chosen for the study guides, quizzes and test. If teachers have other ideas/activities they wish to use, they can usually easily be inserted prior to the review lesson.

UNIT OBJECTIVES - *Hamlet*

1. Through reading Shakespeare's *Hamlet* students will see how one man's greed results in at least nine deaths in the tragedy.

2. Students will demonstrate their understanding of the text on four levels: factual, interpretive, critical and personal.

3. Students will see the conflicts of man vs. himself and man vs. man resolved in the tragedy.

4. Students will learn that political struggles for power within a government are a part of any historical era, not just modern times.

5. Students will study the theme of revenge.

6. Students will be exposed to background information about Shakespeare, Elizabethan drama, and *Hamlet*.

7. Students will examine Shakespeare's use of language.

8. Students will be given the opportunity to practice reading aloud and silently to improve their skills in each area.

9. Students will answer questions to demonstrate their knowledge and understanding of the main events and characters in *Hamlet* as they relate to the author's theme development.

10. Students will enrich their vocabularies and improve their understanding of the play through the vocabulary lessons prepared for use in conjunction with the play.

11. The writing assignments in this unit are geared to several purposes:
    a. To have students demonstrate their abilities to inform, to persuade, or to express their own personal ideas
       Note: Students will demonstrate ability to write effectively to <u>inform</u> by developing and organizing facts to convey information. Students will demonstrate the ability to write effectively to <u>persuade</u> by selecting and organizing relevant information, establishing an argumentative purpose, and by designing an appropriate strategy for an identified audience. Students will demonstrate the ability to write effectively to <u>express personal ideas</u> by selecting a form and its appropriate elements.
    b. To check the students' reading comprehension
    c. To make students think about the ideas presented by the play
    d. To encourage logical thinking

READING ASSIGNMENT SHEET - *Hamlet*

Date Assigned	Reading Assignment Act	Completion Date
	I	
	II	
	III	
	IV	
	V	

UNIT OUTLINE - *Hamlet*

1 Library	2 Nonfiction Reports	3 Materials Parts PV Act I	4 Read Act I	5 Read Act I
6 Study ?s Act I Parts Act II PV Act II	7 Read Act II	8 Writing Assignment 1	9 Study ?s Act II Parts Act III PV Act III	10 Read Act III
11 Read Act III	12 Study ?s Act III Parts Act IV PV Act IV	13 Read Act IV	14 Study ?s Act IV Parts Act V PV Act V	15 Read Act V
16 Study ?s Act V Vocabulary	17 Writing Assignment 2	18 Group Activity	19 Discussion	20 Extra Questions
21 Writing Assignment 3	22 Guest Speaker	23 Review	24 Test	

Key: P = Preview Study Questions   V = Vocabulary Work   R = Read

STUDY GUIDE QUESTIONS

SHORT ANSWER STUDY GUIDE QUESTIONS - *Hamlet*

Act One
1. Identify Bernardo, Francisco, Marcellus, Horatio, and King Hamlet.
2. What had Bernardo seen at a prior watch?
3. Why does Marcellus think Horatio should speak to the ghost?
4. What does young Fortinbras want to do?
5. Who do the soldiers/guards want to tell about the ghost?
6. Identify King Claudius, Queen Gertrude, Laertes, and Polonius.
7. Where does Claudius send Cornelius and Voltimand?
8. What does the King tell Hamlet?
9. Hamlet is upset for two reasons. What are they?
10. What news does Horatio bring Hamlet?
11. What does Hamlet decide to do after he hears Horatio's news?
12. What is Laertes' advice to Ophelia?
13. What is Polonius' advice to Laertes?
14. At the end of Scene III, Ophelia agrees to "obey." What will she do?
15. What did the ghost tell Hamlet?
16. Hamlet swears Horatio to two things. What are they?

Act II
1. Where does Polonius send Reynaldo? Why?
2. Why does Polonius think Hamlet is "mad"?
3. Why have Rosencrantz and Guildenstern come to the castle?
4. What is Polonius' plan for testing his theory that Hamlet is love-crazy?
5. Rosencrantz and Guildenstern finally meet with Hamlet, and Hamlet discovers they were sent for by the King. How does Hamlet describe his personal problems to them? What does he tell them?
6. What arrangement does Hamlet make with Player 1?
7. After Rosencrantz and Guildenstern leave Hamlet, what does he basically say in his soliloquy?

Hamlet Short Answer Study Questions Page 2

Act III
1. What message do Rosencrantz and Guildenstern carry to the King? What is the King's response?
2. Hamlet's famous "To be or not to be" soliloquy is in scene one. In a sentence or two paraphrase his main points.
3. Describe Hamlet's tone when he speaks to Ophelia.
4. What do the King and Polonius decide about Hamlet's condition after eavesdropping on Hamlet and Ophelia?
5. Why does Hamlet give instructions to the players?
6. What was the King's reaction to the play, and what did Hamlet and Horatio decide his reaction meant?
7. What message does Rosencrantz deliver from the Queen?
8. The King has Rosencrantz and Guildenstern prepare to do what? Why?
9. Why doesn't Hamlet kill the King when the King is kneeling?
10. How does Polonius die?
11. What would Hamlet have his mother do?

Act IV
1. What does Hamlet think of Rosencrantz and Guildenstern?
2. Why must the King "not put the strong arm on" Hamlet?
3. When the King asks Hamlet where Polonius is, what is Hamlet's answer?
4. What is the content of the letters the King sends with Rosencrantz and Guildenstern to England with Hamlet?
5. What prompts Hamlet to say, "My thoughts be bloody or be nothing worth!"?
6. What has happened to Ophelia?
7. Why does Laertes force his way in? What does he want?
8. What is the content of Hamlet's letter to Horatio?
9. What plan do the King and Laertes discuss to kill Hamlet?
10. What news does the Queen bring Laertes?

Act V
1. Laertes thinks that Ophelia should have a better funeral service. What is the priest's answer?
2. Why does Hamlet jump into Ophelia's grave?
3. What does the King say to Laertes to console him after Laertes and Hamlet are separated?
4. What did Hamlet do to Rosencrantz and Guildenstern?
5. What news does Osric bring Hamlet?
6. What happens to the King, Hamlet, Laertes, and the Queen?
7. Who does Hamlet recommend to the throne?

ANSWER KEY SHORT ANSWER STUDY GUIDE QUESTIONS - *Hamlet*

Act One

1. Identify Bernardo, Francisco, Marcellus, Horatio, and King Hamlet.
    Bernardo, Francisco and Marcellus are guard soldiers at Elsinore.
    Horatio is Hamlet's friend.
    King Hamlet is Hamlet's father who was murdered prior to the beginning of the play.

2. What had Bernardo seen at a prior watch?
    Bernardo had seen King Hamlet's ghost.

3. Why does Marcellus think Horatio should speak to the ghost?
    Horatio was a scholar who should know the proper way to address a ghost.

4. What does young Fortinbras want to do?
    Young Fortinbras wants to regain the lands his father had lost.

5. Who do the soldiers/guards want to tell about the ghost?
    They think Hamlet (King Hamlet's son) should know about the ghost.

6. Identify King Claudius, Queen Gertrude, Laertes, and Polonius.
    King Claudius is King Hamlet's brother, Hamlet's uncle. He came to the throne and married King Hamlet's wife after King Hamlet's death. Queen Gertrude is Hamlet's mother. Laertes is Polonius' son. Polonius is Lord Chamberlain.

7. Where does Claudius send Cornelius and Voltimand?
    He sends them to the King of Norway with letters asking the King to try to keep young Fortinbras from going to battle.

8. What does the King tell Hamlet?
    He tells Hamlet that Hamlet should not grieve so deeply for his father's death; it is time to think of other things. He says he wants Hamlet to think of him as his father and to remain at cheerful Elsinore for a while longer.

9. Hamlet is upset for two reasons. What are they?
    His father has died, and his uncle has married his mother less than two months after his father's death. It was not a respectable period of time to wait, besides which the marriage in Hamlet's time was considered incestuous.

10. What news does Horatio bring Hamlet?
    Horatio tells Hamlet of King Hamlet's ghost.

11. What does Hamlet decide to do after he hears Horatio's news?
    He decides to go on watch with the guards at midnight in hopes of seeing the ghost himself.

12. What is Laertes' advice to Ophelia?
    He warns her to stay away from Hamlet and tells her to protect her virtue.

13. What is Polonius' advice to Laertes?
    Polonius tells Laertes to not always voice his thoughts, to be familiar but not vulgar, to hold on to his closest friends, to beware of getting into quarrels, to listen to everyone but not to always give advice, to listen to others' opinions without always judging them, to buy good clothes, to not be a borrower or lender, and above all else, to his own self be true.

14. At the end of Scene III, Ophelia agrees to "obey." What will she do?
    She agrees to obey Polonius' wish that she would stay away from Hamlet and reject his affections.

15. What did the ghost tell Hamlet?
    The ghost told Hamlet that King Hamlet was murdered by Claudius, and it asked Hamlet to avenge the murder.

16. Hamlet swears Horatio to two things. What are they?
    He swears him to secrecy about the events of this evening (seeing the ghost) and to go along with him should he pretend to be crazy.

Act II
1. Where does Polonius send Reynaldo? Why?
    Polonius sends Reynaldo to Paris to spy on Laertes and to take him money and messages.

2. Why does Polonius think Hamlet is "mad"?
    He thinks Ophelia's rejections have been too much for Hamlet, that Hamlet is love-sick.

3. Why have Rosencrantz and Guildenstern come to the castle?
    They have come to find out why Hamlet is acting so strangely and to report their findings to the King.

4. What is Polonius' plan for testing his theory that Hamlet is love-crazy?
    He wants to have Hamlet meet Ophelia. He (Polonius) will hide and eavesdrop on the conversation to determine whether or not Hamlet is love-sick.

5. Rosencrantz and Guildenstern finally meet with Hamlet, and Hamlet discovers they were sent for by the King. How does Hamlet describe his personal problems to them? What does he tell them?

   Hamlet basically says that he thought the world was wonderful and man was the most wonderful part of the world, but now he finds that things are not wonderful. He finds no delight in man or woman.

6. What arrangement does Hamlet make with Player 1?

   He arranges to have several of his own lines put into the play (to make the action of the play as closely related to the actual events of his father's murder as possible).

7. After Rosencrantz and Guildenstern leave Hamlet, what does he basically say in his soliloquy?

   He thinks himself a coward for not getting right to the revenge.

Act III

1. What message do Rosencrantz and Guildenstern carry to the King? What is the King's response?

   They tell him Hamlet wishes the King and Queen to see the play. The King gladly accepts.

2. Hamlet's famous "To be or not to be" soliloquy is in scene one. In a sentence or two paraphrase his main points.

   He is pondering whether a miserable life is better than the unknown of death.

3. Describe Hamlet's tone when he speaks to Ophelia.

   He is really quite rude and aggressive.

4. What do the King and Polonius decide about Hamlet's condition after eavesdropping on Hamlet and Ophelia?

   They decide he is not love-sick; rather, he has some other trouble deep in his soul.

5. Why does Hamlet give instructions to the players?

   Hamlet does not want the parts to be over-acted. He wants it to appear as natural and as real as possible so it will hit home to the King.

6. What was the King's reaction to the play, and what did Hamlet and Horatio decide his reaction meant?

   The King got up and called for the lights. Hamlet and Horatio were convinced that the ghost was right, that Claudius had murdered King Hamlet.

7. What message does Rosencrantz deliver from the Queen?

   He told Hamlet that the Queen wanted to see him.

8. The King has Rosencrantz and Guildenstern prepare to do what? Why?
    He has them prepare to take Hamlet to England. Claudius is beginning to feel threatened by Hamlet, and he wants him away from Elsinore. In fact, he wants Hamlet dead.

9. Why doesn't Hamlet kill the King when the King is kneeling?
    Hamlet wants the King to die without a chance for a last confession, as his father died. He thinks if the King is praying, he may not be in sin enough to get eternal punishment.

10. How does Polonius die?
    Polonius is in the Queen's room while she and Hamlet are talking. He hides behind the tapestry but makes some noise. Hamlet runs through the tapestry with his sword (actually thinking Claudius might be there), killing Polonius.

11. What would Hamlet have his mother do?
    He wants her to at least not sleep with the King.

Act IV
1. What does Hamlet think of Rosencrantz and Guildenstern?
    He uses the word "sponge" to describe them, saying they soak up the King's words, commands and gifts. He thinks they are weak and not smart enough to see that they are being used by the King.

2. Why must the king "not put the strong arm on" Hamlet?
    Hamlet's mother truly loves him and would want no harm to come to him, and the people of Denmark love him and would be uneasy if something would happen to him.

3. When the King asks Hamlet where Polonius is, what is Hamlet's answer?
    First he says Polonius is "not where he eats, but where he is eaten." Then he later tells the King to look for him in Heaven, and if he can't find Polonius there, to go to "the other place" (hell) himself.

4. What is the content of the letters the King sends with Rosencrantz and Guildenstern to England with Hamlet?
    The King wants Hamlet to be killed as soon as he reaches England.

5. What prompts Hamlet to say, "My thoughts be bloody or be nothing worth!"?
    He realizes his father has been murdered, his uncle is a murderer, his mother is living in an incestuous marriage, and the soldiers he has just seen are going to kill each other over a little piece of land which is not worth anything.

6. What has happened to Ophelia?
    Ophelia has gone crazy.

7. Why does Laertes force his way in? What does he want?
    Laertes wants revenge for his father's death.

8. What is the content of Hamlet's letter to Horatio?
    He explains that he escaped from Rosencrantz and Guildenstern onto a pirate ship. He is a prisoner, but is being treated well because the pirates want favors from him. He wants Horatio to give letters he has written to the King and Queen and then to come to see him as quickly as possible.

10. What plan do the King and Laertes discuss to kill Hamlet?
    They plan to set up a duel between Laertes and Hamlet in which Laertes will honorably kill Hamlet, or if Hamlet lives, the King will poison him.

11. What news does the Queen bring Laertes?
    She tells him that Ophelia is dead; she has drowned.

Act V
1. Laertes thinks that Ophelia should have a better funeral service. What is the priest's answer?
    The priest more or less says that Ophelia is lucky to be getting as nice of a funeral as she is, considering the nature of her death.

2. Why does Hamlet jump into Ophelia's grave?
    He shows that his sorrow is as great as Laertes'.

3. What does the King say to Laertes to console him after Laertes and Hamlet are separated?
    He tells Laertes not to worry, that he (Laertes) will soon have the appropriate time and place to kill Hamlet, and that one way or another, Hamlet will die.

4. What did Hamlet do to Rosencrantz and Guildenstern?
    Hamlet replaced their letters (which called for Hamlet's execution) with letters which called for the execution of Rosencrantz and Guildenstern.

5. What news does Osric bring Hamlet?
    He tells Hamlet of the wager the King has made on Hamlet's behalf in a contest between Laertes and Hamlet.

6. What happens to the King, Hamlet, Laertes, and the Queen?
    The King is run through and killed by Hamlet. Hamlet is killed by the poison on Laertes' sword. Laertes is killed by the poison on his own sword. The Queen is poisoned and killed by the drink the King had prepared for Hamlet.

7. Who does Hamlet recommend to the throne?
    Hamlet recommends young Fortinbras.

MULTIPLE CHOICE STUDY GUIDE/QUIZ QUESTIONS - *Hamlet*

ACT ONE
1. - 5. Match the characters and the descriptions.

1. ___ Bernardo   A. Murdered prior to the beginning of the play.
2. ___ Marcellus   B. Guard at Elsinore
3. ___ Horatio   C. Hamlet's friend
4. ___ King Hamlet
5. ___ Francisco

6. What had Bernardo seen at a prior watch?
    A. He had seen Horatio and Marcellus meeting secretly in a grove of
       trees. He was suspicious.
    B. He had seen King Hamlet's ghost.
    C. He had seen Hamlet crying and acting crazed.
    D. He had seen the Queen in the arms of an unknown suitor.

7. Why does Marcellus think Horatio should speak to the ghost?
    A. Marcellus thinks Horatio should speak to the ghost because Horatio is the most
       religious of them.
    B. Marcellus thinks Horatio should speak to the ghost because he is the only one
       who does not believe in ghosts, so he is the only one who is not afraid.
    C. Marcellus thinks Horatio should speak to the ghost because he is a scholar and
       should know the proper way to address a ghost.
    D. Marcellus thinks Horatio should speak to the ghost because his parents are dead;
       he may have more influence with the ghost.

8. What does young Fortinbras want to do?
    A. Fortinbras wants to conquer Denmark.
    B. Fortinbras wants to receive payment from Hamlet.
    C. Fortinbras wants to avenge his father's death by killing Hamlet.
    D. Fortinbras wants to regain the lands his father had lost.

9. Who do the soldiers/guards want to tell about the ghost?
    A. They want to tell Hamlet (King Hamlet's son).
    B. They want to tell the Queen.
    C. They want to tell the priests.
    D. They want to tell the Commander of the Guards.

Hamlet Multiple Choice Study/Quiz Questions Page 2

10. - 13. Match the characters and the descriptions.
   10. ___King Claudius   A. the son of the Lord Chamberlain
   11. ___Gertrude   B. Hamlet's mother.
   12. ___Laertes   C. the Lord Chamberlain.
   13. ___Polonius   D. Hamlet's uncle.

14. Where does Claudius send Cornelius and Voltimand?
   A. He sends them to Sweden for reinforcements.
   B. He sends them to England to ask for money.
   C. He sends them to Norway to ask the King to keep Fortinbras from going to battle.
   D. He sends them to Rome to get the Pope's blessing for the upcoming battle.

15. What does the King tell Hamlet?
   A. He suggests that Hamlet think about going to England to go to the University at Cambridge.
   B. He tells Hamlet to stop grieving for his father's death, and to think of him as his father.
   C. He tells Hamlet that he should go on a pilgrimage to honor his father.
   D. He tells him that the Queen never really loved King Hamlet, and is only pretending to grieve for him. She secretly loved Claudius all along.

16. Hamlet is upset for two reasons. What are they?
   A. His mother has been ignoring him, and his fiancée has cancelled the wedding plans.
   B. His father has died, and his uncle has declared war on Fortinbras.
   C. He wants to travel for about a year, but he is afraid to leave his mother because she has been acting strangely since the King's death.
   D. His father has died, and his uncle has married his mother less than two months after his father's death.

17. What news does Horatio bring Hamlet?
   A. Horatio tells Hamlet of a great plague that has come upon the land.
   B. Horatio tells Hamlet that his mother has been excommunicated.
   C. Horatio tells Hamlet that Fortinbras is on the way with his army.
   D. Horatio tells Hamlet about King Hamlet's ghost.

18. What does Hamlet decide to do after he hears Horatio's news?
   A. Hamlet decides to go to confession and communion.
   B. He decides to have the doctor examine his mother.
   C. Hamlet decides to go on watch with the guards at midnight to verify Horatio's news.
   D. He decides to ready his army for battle.

Hamlet Multiple Choice Study/Quiz Questions Page 3

19. What is Laertes' advice to Ophelia?
    A. He warns her to stay away from Hamlet and tells her to protect her virtue.
    B. He tells her to take time to look over all of the young men before she makes a choice.
    C. He tells her she would be better off going to a convent than marrying any one of her suitors.
    D. He tells her that Polonius is secretly in love with her.

20. Polonius gives a lot of advice to Laertes. Which of these statements is **not** part of that advice?
    A. "Costly thy habit as thy purse can buy, but not expressed in fancy; rich; not gaudy; For the apparel oft proclaims the man."
    B. "Keep you in the rear of your affection. Out of the shot and danger of desire."
    C. "To thine own self be true."
    D. "Neither a borrower nor a lender be, For loan oft loses both itself and friend, And borrowing dulls the edge of husbandry."

21. At the end of Scene III, Ophelia agrees to obey Polonius' wish. What will she do?
    A. She will marry Fortinbras.
    B. She will go into a convent for a year of prayer.
    C. She will stay away from Hamlet and reject his affections.
    D. She will befriend the Queen to spy on her.

22. What did the ghost tell Hamlet?
    A. The ghost told Hamlet that King Hamlet was murdered by Claudius, and it asked Hamlet to avenge the murder.
    B. The ghost told Hamlet that he was not really the son of King Hamlet. The Queen had lied, and Hamlet was really the son of Claudius.
    C. The ghost told Hamlet that Fortinbras is the rightful ruler, and asks Hamlet to help him gain the throne.
    D. The ghost tells Hamlet that he should take his mother and flee to Sweden, where they will be safe.

23. Hamlet swears Horatio to two things. What are they?
    A. Hamlet asks Horatio to promise to protect his mother, and to defend the country against Fortinbras.
    B. Hamlet asks Horatio to promise to attend Mass for him everyday for a year if he dies, and to marry Ophelia.
    C. Hamlet asks Horatio not to reveal the events of the evening, and to go along with him (Hamlet) if he pretends to be crazy.
    D. Hamlet asks Horatio to defend him in battle, and to kill Claudius if he (Hamlet) does not do it first.

Hamlet Multiple Choice Study/Quiz Questions Page 4

ACT TWO

24. Where does Polonius send Reynaldo?
    A. Polonius sends Reynaldo to London to offer the King money in return for soldiers.
    B. Polonius sends Reynaldo to Paris to spy on Laertes and to take him money and messages.
    C. Polonius sends Reynaldo to the castle to take care of Hamlet.
    D. Polonius sends Reynaldo to Sweden, Finland, and Norway to see who will give Hamlet and the Queen asylum if they need it.

25. Why does Polonius think Hamlet is mad?
    A. He thinks Ophelia's rejections have been too much for Hamlet, that Hamlet is lovesick.
    B. He thinks Hamlet has been dabbling in witchcraft, and that it is affecting his mind.
    C. He thinks Hamlet is angry because he has not become King. His anger and jealousy are driving him mad.
    D. He thinks Hamlet realizes now that the King never really loved him. Now that the King is dead, there is nowhere to release his frustration. He is turning it inward, which makes him appear mad.

26. Why have Rosencrantz and Guildenstern come to the castle?
    A. They have come to help the Queen redecorate in a manner suitable to Claudius.
    B. They have come to tutor Hamlet so that he can go on to the University in Paris or London.
    C. They are master soldiers who have come to prepare the troops for battle.
    D. They have come to find out why Hamlet is acting so strangely and to report their findings to the King.

27. What is Polonius' plan for testing his theory about Hamlet's madness?
    A. He wants to stage a duel and see if Hamlet is mentally aware enough to fight.
    B. He wants the most famous doctors to be brought from all over Europe to observe and study Hamlet, then to make a diagnosis and treatment plan.
    C. He wants to have Hamlet meet Ophelia. He (Polonius) will hide and eavesdrop on the conversation.
    D. He wants the priest to come from Rome to perform an exorcism on Hamlet.

Hamlet Multiple Choice Study/Quiz Questions Page 5

28. Rosencrantz and Guildenstern finally meet with Hamlet, and Hamlet discovers they were sent for by the King. How does Hamlet describe his personal problems to them?
    A. He compares himself to an erupting volcano.
    B. He tells them he used to think the world was wonderful, but now he finds differently, and he has no delight in man or woman.
    C. Hamlet has written a poem that he reads to them, describing his sorrows.
    D. He cries and takes them into his confidence, hoping they will align themselves with him against the King.

29. What arrangement does Hamlet make with Player 1?
    A. He arranges to trade places with the player during the last act of the play.
    B. He arranges to have the lights turned on and the play ruined in the middle of the performance.
    C. He arranges to have several of his own lines put into the play.
    D. He arranges to have the player pay extra attention to the Queen, to get the King jealous.

30. After Rosencrantz and Guildenstern leave Hamlet, what does he basically say in his soliloquy?
    A. He thinks himself a coward for not getting right to the revenge.
    B. He knows he is about to commit a mortal sin, and he begs God's forgiveness.
    C. He believes that love conquers all, and he resolves to be even more loving toward those he dislikes.
    D. He is angry at his father. He says that if King Hamlet had been stronger, he never would have let Claudius kill him.

Hamlet Multiple Choice Study/Quiz Questions Page 6

ACT THREE

31. What message do Rosencrantz and Guildenstern carry to the King and Queen? What is their response?
    A. They tell them Hamlet wants the King to order Ophelia to marry him. The King refuses.
    B. They tell them Hamlet is having a special Mass said for his dead father. He asks them to come. The Queen accepts, but the King refuses.
    C. They tell them Hamlet wants to go off on a long journey, on foot, by himself. The Queen objects, but the King thinks it is a good idea.
    They tell them Hamlet wishes the King and Queen to see a play that night. They both accept.

32. Hamlet's famous "To be or not to be" soliloquy is in Scene One. Which of the following paraphrases his main points?
    A. He questions whether love, either romantic or family love, is worth all of the pain it causes.
    B. He is pondering whether a miserable life is better than the unknown of the death.
    C. He questions whether peace of mind is a good substitute for material wealth.
    D. He questions the traditions about succession to the throne in Denmark. He feels that either he or his mother should be the rightful successor to his dead father.

33. Describe Hamlet's tone when he speaks to Ophelia.
    A. He is kind and loving.
    B. He is patronizing and sarcastic.
    C. He is rude and aggressive.
    D. He is meek and fearful.

34. What do the King and Polonius decide about Hamlet's condition after eavesdropping on Hamlet and Ophelia?
    A. They decide he is love-sick, and the only cure is to find him another love.
    B. They decide he is not love-sick; rather; he has some other trouble deep in his soul.
    C. They decide his father's death has left him troubled.
    D. They decide he's not sick at all; he's just being a spoiled brat throwing a tantrum.

Hamlet Multiple Choice Study/Quiz Questions Page 7

35. Why does Hamlet give instructions to the players?
    A. In his madness, he believes that he is really a great actor, not the Prince of Denmark.
    B. He is helping them remember their lines, because he does not want to disappoint his mother when she watches the play.
    C. He is merely showing off his superiority, to keep in character with his masquerade of being mad.
    D. He does not want the parts to be over-acted. He wants it to appear as natural and as real as possible, so it will hit home to the King.

36. What was the King's reaction to the play, and what did Hamlet and Horatio decide his reaction meant?
    A. The King had no reaction to the play. They decided it meant they were wrong, and that he was innocent after all.
    B. The King laughed and laughed. They decided he didn't really get the point, and they would have to be more direct the next time.
    C. The King got up and called for the lights. They were convinced that the ghost had been correct.
    D. The King clenched his teeth and gripped the arms of his chair, but said nothing. They thought they were on the right track, but would need to do something else to force the King into making a confession.

37. What message does Rosencrantz deliver to Hamlet from the Queen?
    A. She is angry and won't speak to him for one month.
    B. She wants to see him.
    C. She is arranging for him to have dinner with a girl she thinks he will like.
    D. She wants him to go to Norway immediately.

38. The King has Rosencrantz and Guildenstern prepare to do what?
    A. They prepare to take Hamlet to England.
    B. They prepare to try and patch things up between Hamlet and Ophelia.
    C. They prepare to help Hamlet write another play. However in this one, the King has written some lines that accuse Hamlet of the murder of his father.
    D. They prepare to capture Hamlet and imprison him.

Hamlet Multiple Choice Study/Quiz Questions Page 8

39. Why doesn't Hamlet kill the King when the King is kneeling?
    A. Hamlet wants his mother to be there to witness the deed.
    B. Hamlet loses heart, and realizes that his father would not have wanted another murder committed.
    C. Hamlet wants the King to die without a chance for a last confession. If he is praying, he may not be in enough sin to get eternal punishment.
    D. He thinks he hears noises in the hallway. He is afraid that someone will see him. He decides to wait until he can be sure they are alone.

40. How does Polonius die?
    A. He and Ophelia are standing on the top of the castle tower, talking. Ophelia becomes enraged and pushes him over the edge.
    B. Polonius is hiding in the Queen's room while she and Hamlet are talking. He makes a noise. Hamlet runs through the tapestry, thinking it may be Claudius, and kills Polonius.
    C. The King decides to get rid of any potential enemies. He sends Rosencrantz and Guildenstern to murder Polonius. They make it look like a suicide.
    D. He realizes Hamlet has been right all along. He kills himself in his grief and remorse.

41. What would Hamlet have his mother do?
    A. He wants her to go to England.
    B. He wants her to stop sleeping with the King.
    C. He wants her to have the marriage annulled by the Church.
    D. He wants her to poison the King at dinner the next night.

Hamlet Multiple Choice Study/Quiz Questions Page 9

ACT IV

42. What does Hamlet think of Rosencrantz and Guildenstern?
    A. He calls them sponges, saying they soak up the King's words, commands and gifts.
    B. He calls them leeches, saying they associate themselves with the King to appear superior to other commoners.
    C. He calls them monsters, saying they are selfish and look for ways to destroy others.
    D. He calls them monkeys, saying they follow the King's orders without thinking.

43. Why must the King "not put the strong arm on" Hamlet?
    A. He is afraid that his soul would be permanently blackened if he committed any more evil deeds.
    B. He is protecting his wife. He thinks that Hamlet might try to hurt her if he is provoked.
    C. He needs to save all of his strength for fighting the enemies from other countries.
    D. Hamlet's mother would not want him harmed. The people of Denmark like him and would be upset if anything happened to him..

44. When the King asks Hamlet where Polonius is, what is Hamlet's answer?
    A. First he says he has "brought the fair body to the chapel." Then he says it is in a place where no harm will come to it.
    B. First he says it is with the other vermin. Then he says it is on its way to England, so as not to desecrate good Danish soil.
    C. First he says it is "not where he eats, but where he is eaten." Then he tells the King to look for him in Heaven, and if he can't find Polonius there, to go to "the other place" (hell) himself.
    D. First he says Polonius is now "keeping company with my dear dead father." Later he tells the King he has put the body on display in the marketplace for all the people to see, telling them that this is what happens to those who disobey the King.

45. What is the content of the letters the King sends with Rosencrantz and Guildenstern to England with Hamlet?
    A. The King wants Hamlet to be killed as soon as he reaches England.
    B. The King sends money to the King of England to pay for Hamlet's upkeep for one year.
    C. The King sends a document saying that Hamlet is mad, and asking that he be imprisoned in the Tower of London until he regains his sanity.
    D. It is a letter thanking the King of England for his help, and inviting him and his wife to visit Denmark the following spring.

Hamlet Multiple Choice Study/Quiz Questions Page 10

46. What prompts Hamlet to say, "My thoughts be bloody or be nothing worth!"?
    A. He feels guilty for killing Polonius.
    B. He realizes that his father has been murdered, his uncle is a murderer, his mother is living in an incestuous marriage, and the soldiers he has just seen are going to kill each other over a little piece of land which is not worth anything.
    C. He decides to offer Rosencrantz and Guildenstern more money than the King is giving them, in the hopes that they will turn traitor on the King and murder him for Hamlet. He realizes that he is committing a wrong, but decides to do it anyway.
    D. He realizes that he has been thinking about death and destruction almost constantly. He feels sad, and wonders if he will ever again be able to think peaceful thoughts.

47. What has happened to Ophelia?
    A. She has married another man, chosen by her father.
    B. She has gone to a convent in Norway.
    C. She has defied her father and announced that she is going to England to be with Hamlet.
    D. She has gone crazy.

48. Why does Laertes force his way in? What does he want?
    A. He wants to marry Ophelia.
    B. He wants to kidnap the Queen and hold her for ransom.
    C. He wants to avenge his father's death.
    D. He wants to be given the title to his father's lands.

49. What is the content of Hamlet's letter to Horatio?
    A. He says he has escaped from Rosencrantz and Guildenstern onto a pirate ship, where he is being well treated. He asks Horatio to give letters to the King and Queen, and then to come to see him as quickly as possible.
    B. He tells him about his old friend Yorick.
    C. He expresses his regrets about the way he has treated Ophelia, but says that he has acted this way for a greater good.
    D. He asks Horatio to talk to the Queen for him; he thinks she might listen to Horatio.

Hamlet Multiple Choice Study/Quiz Questions Page 11

50. What plan do the King and Laertes discuss to kill Hamlet?
    A. They will go to see him, disguised as beggars. Then they will rob him and kill him.
    B. They plan to set up a duel between Laertes and Hamlet. Either Laertes will honorably kill Hamlet, or, if he survives, the King will poison him.
    C. They plan to go to him and escort him back to Denmark. On the way, they will stage a shipwreck. They will leave Hamlet in the water to perish, and they will be rescued by another ship.
    B. They plan to force Horatio to do it. If he refuses they will kill all the members of his family.

51. The Queen tells Laertes that Ophelia is dead. How did she die?
    A. She has taken poison.
    B. She has died of a broken heart.
    C. She has fallen on her own knife.
    D. She has drowned.

Hamlet Multiple Choice Study/Quiz Questions Page 12

ACT V

52. Laertes thinks that Ophelia should have a better funeral service. What is the priest's answer.
    A. He says there is no one to pay for it, since Polonius is already dead.
    B. He agrees and sets about preparing one.
    C. He says she is lucky to be getting as nice of a funeral as she is, considering the nature of her death.
    D. He says that women are inferior beings and only deserve very simple funerals.

53. Why does Hamlet jump into Ophelia's grave?
    A. He wants to make sure that she is really dead.
    B. He shows that his sorrow is as great as Laertes'.
    C. He wants everyone to think he is still mad.
    D. He wants to be buried alive so he can be with her forever.

54. What does the King say to Laertes to console him after Laertes and Hamlet are separated?
    A. The King tells Laertes not to worry, that he (Laertes) will soon have the appropriate time and place to kill Hamlet.
    B. He offers Laertes money and a piece of land as consolation.
    C. He tells Laertes he will have the priest say a special prayer to make sure Ophelia's soul goes to heaven.
    D. He tells Laertes that he (the King) will exile Hamlet instead of killing him.

55. What does Hamlet do to Rosencrantz and Guildenstern?
    A. He pays a group of thugs to beat them and leave them for dead.
    B. He offers them money and reminds them that the three of them used to be friends. He asks them to stay with him.
    C. He arranged for them to be kidnapped and taken to Poland.
    D. He replaced their letters (which called for Hamlet's execution) with letters which called for their executions.

56. What news does Osric bring Hamlet?
    A. The King has forgiven him and offered him safe passage.
    B. The King and Queen are expecting a child.
    C. The King has made a wager on Hamlet's behalf in a contest between Laertes and Hamlet.
    D. The King has confessed to the murder of King Hamlet, and has renounced the throne. Hamlet is the new King of Denmark.

Hamlet Multiple Choice Study/Quiz Questions Page 13

57.-60. What happens to each of these characters?

57. ___ The King		A. Drinks a poisoned beverage
58. ___ Hamlet		B. Is run through with Hamlet's sword.
59. ___ Laertes		C. Is killed by the poison on his opponent's sword
60. ___ The Queen		D. Is killed by the poison on his own sword

ANSWER KEY - MULTIPLE CHOICE STUDY/QUIZ QUESTIONS
Hamlet

Act I	Act II	Act III	Act IV	Act V
1. B	24. B	31. D	42. A	52. C
2. B	25. A	32. B	43. D	53. B
3. C	26. D	33. C	44. C	54. A
4. A	27. C	34. B	45. A	55. D
5. B	28. B	35. D	46. B	56. C
6. B	29. C	36. C	47. D	57. B
7. C	30. A	37. B	48. C	58. C
8. D		38. A	49. A	59. D
9. A		39. C	50. B	60. A
10. D		40. B	51. D	
11. B		41. B		
12. A				
13. C				
14. C				
15. B				
16. D				
17. D				
18. C				
19. A				
20. B				
21. C				
22. A				
23. C				

PREREADING VOCABULARY WORKSHEETS

VOCABULARY - *Hamlet*

Act 1

1. ... that this <u>portentous</u> figure/ Comes armed through our watch

_____

2. - 3. ... it is as the air <u>invulnerable</u>. /And our vain blows <u>malicious</u> mockery,

_____

4. But you must know your father lost a father. / That father lost, lost his, and the survivor bound in <u>filial</u> obligation for some term.

_____

5. The chariest maid is <u>prodigal</u> enough/ If she unmask her beauty to the moon.

_____

6. ... it went hand in hand even with the <u>vow</u> /I made to her in marriage

_____

7. O most <u>pernicious</u> woman!/ O villain, villain, smiling damned villain!

_____

8. Or by pronouncing of some doubtful phrase,/ \As ..."If we list to speak." or "There be, an if they might."/ ...Or such <u>ambiguous</u> giving out,

_____

Part II: Determining the Meaning -- Match the vocabulary words to their definitions.

___ 1. portentous
___ 2. invulnerable
___ 3. malicious
___ 4. filial
___ 5. prodigal
___ 6. vow
___ 7. pernicious
___ 8. ambiguous

A. An earnest promise.
B. Rashly or wastefully extravagant.
C. The relationship of child or offspring to parent.
D. Open to more than one interpretation..
E. Immune to attack; impregnable; impossible to damage, injure, or wound.
F. Full of unspecifiable significance; exciting wonder and awe.
G. Spiteful
H. Deadly; destructive.

Hamlet Vocabulary Worksheet Page 2
Act II

9. This is the very ecstasy of love./ Whose violent property for does itself/ And leads the will to desperate undertakings/ As oft as any passion under heaven/ That does <u>afflict</u> our natures.

___

10. ... it is common for the younger sort/ To lack <u>discretion</u>.

___

11. ... I <u>entreat</u> you both...That you vouchsafe your rest here in our Court/ Some little time,

___

12. And I <u>beseech</u> you instantly to visit/ My too much changed son.

___

13. I will leave him, and suddenly <u>contrive</u> the means of meeting between him and my daughter.

___

14. What a piece of work is a man!.../ The <u>paragon</u> of animals!

___

15. The <u>appurtenance</u> of welcome is fashion and ceremony.

___

16. After your death you were better have a bad <u>epitaph</u> than their ill report while you live.

___

Part II: Determining the Meaning -- Match the vocabulary words to their definitions.

___ 9. afflict   A. Ability or power to decide responsibly.
___ 10. discretion   B. To make an earnest request of.
___ 11. entreat   C. Something added to another, more important thing; an appendage.
___ 12. beseech   D. To inflict grievous physical or mental suffering on.
___ 13. contrive   E. An inscription on a tombstone in memory of the one buried there.
___ 14. paragon   F. A model of excellence or perfection of a kind.
___ 15. appurtenance G. To address an earnest or urgent request to; implore.
___ 16. epitaph   H. To plan with cleverness or ingenuity

Hamlet Vocabulary Worksheet Page 3
Act III

17. And blest are those/ Whose blood and judgment are so well commingled / That they are not a pipe for fortune's finger

_____

18. ...'Tis a knavish piece of/ work, but what o' that?

_____

19. "Tis now the very witching time of night,/ When churchyards yawn and Hell itself breathes out/ Contagion to this world.

_____

20. Be soft as sinews of the newborn babe!

_____

21. . . . Heaven's face doth glow...With heated visage, as against the doom,

_____

22. Do not look upon me/Lest with this piteous action you convert/ My stern effects.

_____

23. . . . but Heaven hath pleased it so,/ To punish me with this, and this with me,/ That I must be their scourge and minister.

_____

Part II: Determining the Meaning -- Match the vocabulary words to their definitions.

___ 17. commingled		A. Tendons; muscles.
___ 18. knavish		B. A means of inflicting severe suffering, vengeance, or punishment.
___ 19. contagion		C. Blended.
___ 20. sinews		D. Unprincipled.
___ 21. visage		E. Demanding or arousing pity.
___ 22. piteous		F. Harmful or corrupting influence.
___ 23. scourge		G. The face or facial expression.

Hamlet Vocabulary Worksheet Page 4

Act IV

24. ... But, like the owner of a foul disease,/ To keep it from <u>divulging</u> let it feed/ Even on the pith of life.

_____

25. ... My soul is full of <u>discord</u> and dismay.

_____

26. ... Besides to be demanded of a sponge! What <u>replication</u> should be made by the son of a king?

_____

27. A certain <u>convocation</u> of politic worms are e'en at/ him

_____

28. ... And let all sleep while to my shame I see/ The <u>imminent</u> death of twenty thousand men

_____

29. ... O my dear Gertrude, this,/ Like to a murdering piece in many places/ Gives me a <u>superfluous</u> death.

_____

30. ... We should do when we would; for this "would" changes/ And hath <u>abatements</u> and delays as many

_____

Part II: Determining the Meaning -- Match the vocabulary words to their definitions.

    ___ 24. divulging   A. Reductions in amount, degree, or intensity.
    ___ 25. discord   B. Being beyond what is required or sufficient.
    ___ 26. replication   C. A reply to an answer; a rejoinder.
    ___ 27. convocation   D. About to occur; impending.
    ___ 28. imminent   E. Becoming known.
    ___ 29. superfluous   F. Tension or strife.
    ___ 30. abatements   G. Assembly.

Hamlet Vocabulary Worksheet Page 5

Act V

31. . . . To what base uses we may return, Horatio!

___

32. . . . I tell thee churlish priest,/ A ministering angel shall my sister be/ When thou liest howling.

___

33. . . . An earnest conjuration from the King,

___

34. . . . . Sir, his definement suffers no perdition in you

___

35. But in the verity of extolment I take him to be a soul of great article,

___

36. But in my terms of honor/ I stand aloof and will no reconcilement

___

37. . . . Absent thee from felicity a while,/ And in this harsh world draw thy breath in pain/ To tell my story.

___

38. . . . So shall you hear/ Of carnal, bloody, and unnatural acts,

___

Part II: Determining the Meaning -- Match the vocabulary words to their definitions.

   ___ 31. base   A. Difficult to work with.
   ___ 32. churlish   B. High praise.
   ___ 33. conjuration   C. Of or relating to the body or flesh; bodily.
   ___ 34. perdition   D. Great happiness; bliss.
   ___ 35. extolment   E. Loss of the soul; eternal damnation.
   ___ 36. aloof   F. The lowest or bottom part.
   ___ 37. felicity   G. Influence or effect by a supernatural power.
   ___ 38. carnal   H. Distant physically or emotionally.

KEY: VOCABULARY WORKSHEETS - *Hamlet*

Act I	Act II	Act III	Act IV	Act V
1. F	9. D	17. C	24. E	31. F
2. E	10. A	18. D	25. F	32. A
3. G	11. B	19. F	26. C	33. G
4. C	12. G	20. A	27. G	34. E
5. B	13. H	21. G	28. D	35. B
6. A	14. F	22. E	29. B	36. H
7. H	15. C	23. B	30. A	37. D
8. D	16. E			38. C

DAILY LESSONS

LESSON ONE

Objectives
1. To gather background information
2. To give students the opportunity to fulfill their nonfiction reading assignment
3. To give students practice using the resources in the library
4. To distribute the materials which will be used in the unit

NOTE: If you have already done the background work for Shakespeare and *Hamlet*, (have already done another play by Shakespeare, for example) see the Alternate Introductory Activity in the Unit Resource Materials section of this unit.

Activity #1

Distribute the materials which will be used in this unit. Explain in detail how students are to use these materials.

Study Guides Students should read the study guide questions for each reading assignment prior to beginning the reading assignment to get a feeling for what events and ideas are important in the section they are about to read. After reading the section, students will (as a class or individually) answer the questions to review the important events and ideas from that section of the play. Students should keep the study guides as study materials for the unit test.

Vocabulary Prior to reading a reading assignment, students will do vocabulary work related to the section of the play they are about to read. Following the completion of the reading of the play, there will be a vocabulary review of all the words used in the vocabulary assignments. Students should keep their vocabulary work as study materials for the unit test.

Reading Assignment Sheet You need to fill in the reading assignment sheet to let students know by when their reading has to be completed. You can either write the assignment sheet up on a side blackboard or bulletin board and leave it there for students to see each day, or you can "ditto" copies for each student to have. In either case, you should advise students to become very familiar with the reading assignments so they know what is expected of them.

Extra Activities Center The Extra Activities page of this unit contains suggestions for an extra library of related plays and articles in your classroom as well as crossword and word search puzzles. Make an extra activities center in your room where you will keep these materials for students to use. (Bring the books and articles in from the library and keep several copies of the puzzles on hand.) Explain to students that these materials are available for students to use when they finish reading assignments or other class work early.

<u>Nonfiction Assignment Sheet</u> Explain to students that they each are to read at least one non-fiction piece from the in-class library at some time during the unit. Students will fill out a nonfiction assignment sheet after completing the reading to help you evaluate their reading experiences and to help the students think about and evaluate their own reading experiences.

<u>Books</u> Each school has its own rules and regulations regarding student use of school books. Advise students of the procedures that are normal for your school.

<u>Activity #2</u>
Take students to your school library. Distribute the Research Assignment Sheet. Discuss the directions in detail, and give students ample time to complete the assignment. Depending on how quickly your students work, you may also need to spend part of the class period for Lesson Two in the library.

RESEARCH ASSIGNMENT - *Hamlet*

Purposes
1. To give you some background information about Shakespeare, *Hamlet* and the historical era in which the play was written and performed
2. To help you fulfill the nonfiction reading assignment which is a part of this unit

Assignment

Use the resources of your library and/or media center to find out as much as you can about the topic your group has been assigned. Take notes so you remember what you have read, seen or heard. After you have collected your information, get together with the other members of your group to compile a "Fact Sheet," an outline of the facts you have gathered. You will be asked to give an oral report to share your information with the rest of your classmates so that everyone in your class will have information about each of the topics assigned. The "Fact Sheet" you prepare will be the basis of your oral report and, if duplicated, will serve as a study guide for you and your classmates.

If you wish, you may use this assignment to fulfill your nonfiction reading assignment for this unit. If you choose to do so, be sure to fill out your Nonfiction Reading Assignment Sheet.

Group 1: Research Shakespeare. Pretend as if you had to write a book about Shakespeare (a biography). Include information about his personal life, professional life, important events and influences in his life, and any topics of controversy surrounding his life.

Group 2: Research British History 1550-1650. What was going on in Britain during the time just before, during and just after Shakespeare lived? Who were the rulers? What was the political atmosphere? What were the people concerned about? How did the people live? Answer these kinds of questions in your report.

Group 3: Research World History 1550-1650. What was going on in the rest of the world (besides Britain) during this period?

Group 4: Research *Hamlet*. What is the play about? Why is it famous? What do critics say about it? Has there been more than one version of the play? Which one(s) are most often performed? Why? Which is/was the best production of the play? What difficulties are there in performing the play (if any)?

Getting Started

There are many sources of information for your research. Books, periodicals (magazines & journals), films/filmstrips/videos, and encyclopedias are some of the most commonly used research materials. Each member of your group should use a different source of materials. For example, one member should look for books, another should look for articles in periodicals, etc.

NONFICTION ASSIGNMENT SHEET
(To be completed after reading the required nonfiction article)

Name _____ Date _____

Title of Nonfiction Read _____

Written By _____ Publication Date _____

I. Factual Summary: Write a short summary of the piece you read.

II. Vocabulary
    1. With which vocabulary words in the piece did you encounter some degree of difficulty?

    2. How did you resolve your lack of understanding with these words?

III. Interpretation: What was the main point the author wanted you to get from reading his work?

IV. Criticism
    1. With which points of the piece did you agree or find easy to accept? Why?

    2. With which points of the piece did you disagree or find difficult to believe? Why?

V. Personal Response: What do you think about this piece? OR How does this piece influence your ideas?

LESSON TWO

Objectives
1. To give students time to finish their research
2. To give students time to compile their fact sheets
3. To evaluate students' research
4. To have students share all the information they have found

Activity #1
Give students ample time to complete their research and compile their research fact sheets.

Activity #2
Have one student from each group give an oral report to the class summarizing the information all the group members found. If you choose, students could just listen instead of taking notes, and you could duplicate the fact sheets for distribution in the next class period. The other alternative is to have students take notes from the class reports so they have study materials.

LESSON THREE

Objectives
1. To assign reading parts for Act I
2. To do the prereading activities for Act I

Activity #1
Explain that because *Hamlet* is a play it is meant to be acted on a stage. If you are not planning a production of the play, explain to students that the next best thing we can do is to read the parts orally. Each person in class will (eventually) have a speaking part to perform. The part does not have to be memorized, but the students' oral reading will be evaluated.

Make the reading part assignments for Act I, which will be read in Lesson Five. (Tell students the day and date that their reading will be done.)

Narrator (stage descriptions and directions; italicized)

Bernardo	Francisco
Horatio	Marcellus
King	Cornelius
Voltimand	Laertes
Polonius	Queen
Hamlet	Ophelia
Ghost	

Activity #3
Prior to reading Act I, students should preview the study questions and do the prereading vocabulary work for Act I. Give students the remainder of this class period to do the prereading work and, if they finish that, to begin practicing their oral reading parts.

LESSONS FOUR AND FIVE

Objectives
1. To read Act I of *Hamlet*
2. To evaluate students' oral reading

Activity

Have students who were assigned to read parts for Act I do so during these class periods. If you have not yet evaluated students' oral reading this marking period, this would be a good opportunity to do so. An Oral Reading Evaluation form is included in this unit for your convenience.

LESSON SIX

Objectives
1. To review the main events and ideas presented in Act I
2. To assign the speaking parts for Act II
3. To do the prereading work for Act II

Activity #1

Give students a few minutes to formulate answers for the study guide questions for Act I, and then discuss the answers to the questions in detail. Write the answers on the board or overhead transparency so students can have the correct answers for study purposes. Note: It is a good practice in public speaking and leadership skills for individual students to take charge of leading the discussions of the study questions. Perhaps a different student could go to the front of the class and lead the discussion each day that the study questions are discussed during this unit. Of course, the teacher should guide the discussion when appropriate and be sure to fill in any gaps the students leave.

Activity #2

Assign the following speaking parts for Act II. (Tell students that they will be reading Act II during the next class period.)

Polonius	Reynaldo
Ophelia	King
Queen	Guildenstern
Rosencrantz	Hamlet
Player 1	Narrator

Activity #3

Prior to reading Act II, students should preview the study questions and do the prereading vocabulary work for Act II. Give students the remainder of this class period to do the prereading work and, if they finish that, to begin practicing their oral reading parts.

ORAL READING EVALUATION - *Hamlet*

Name _____ Class _____ Date _____

SKILL	EXCELLENT	GOOD	AVERAGE	FAIR	POOR
Fluency	5	4	3	2	1
Clarity	5	4	3	2	1
Audibility	5	4	3	2	1
Pronunciation	5	4	3	2	1
_____	5	4	3	2	1
_____	5	4	3	2	1

Total _____ Grade _____

Comments:

LESSON SEVEN

Objectives
    1. To read Act II of *Hamlet*
    2. To evaluate students' oral reading

Activity
    Have students who were assigned to read parts for Act II do so during these class periods. If you have not yet evaluated students' oral reading this marking period, this would be a good opportunity to do so. An Oral Reading Evaluation form is included in this unit for your convenience.

LESSON EIGHT

Objectives
    1. To give students practice writing to inform
    2. To review the background information students researched
    3. To give the teacher the opportunity to evaluate students' writing

Activity
    Distribute Writing Assignment 1. Discuss the directions in detail and give students this class period to do the assignment.

    Follow-Up: After you have graded the assignments, have a writing conference with the students. After the writing conference, allow students to revise their papers using your suggestions and corrections. Give them about three days from the date they receive their papers to complete the revision. I suggest grading the revisions on an A-C-E scale (all revisions well-done, some revisions made, few or no revisions made). This will speed your grading time and still give some credit for the students' efforts.

WRITING ASSIGNMENT #1 - *Hamlet*

PROMPT
Your assignment is to write a complete composition about the background information you researched at the beginning of this unit.

PREWRITING
Start by looking at the notes you took as you were gathering information. Then, look at the fact sheet you and the members of your group compiled. Think of one statement you could make about all this information. That will be the main idea of your paper. Can the information you have gathered be put into categories? (Are there some things that naturally go together?) Is there a logical progression of ideas? (Can your information be put in chronological order? If so, do it.)

DRAFTING
First write a paragraph in which you introduce the topic of your composition. The paragraphs in the body of your composition will all support or explain your main topic. The paragraphs should flow from idea to idea (from category to category, or in chronological order from earliest to latest, etc.). Your final paragraph should include the conclusions you can draw from the information presented and should bring your composition to a close.

PROMPT
When you finish the rough draft of your paper, ask a student who sits near you to read it. After reading your rough draft, he/she should tell you what he/she liked best about your work, which parts were difficult to understand, and ways in which your work could be improved. Reread your paper considering your critic's comments, and make the corrections you think are necessary.

PROOFREADING
Do a final proofreading of your paper double-checking your grammar, spelling, organization, and the clarity of your ideas.

LESSON NINE

Objectives
1. To review the main events and ideas presented in Act II
2. To assign the speaking parts for Act III
3. To do the prereading work for Act III

Activity #1
Give students a few minutes to formulate answers for the study guide questions for Act II, and then discuss the answers to the questions in detail. Write the answers on the board or overhead transparency so students can have the correct answers for study purposes.

Activity #2
Assign the following speaking parts for Act III. (Tell students that they will be reading Act III during the next class period.)

Narrator	Rosencrantz
Guildenstern	Queen
Polonius	Hamlet
Ophelia	Player 1
Horatio	P. King
P. Queen	Lucianus

Activity #3
Prior to reading Act III, students should preview the study questions and do the prereading vocabulary work for Act III. Give students the remainder of this class period to do the prereading work and, if they finish that, to begin practicing their oral reading parts.

LESSONS TEN AND ELEVEN

Objectives
1. To read Act III of *Hamlet*
2. To evaluate students' oral reading

Activity
Have students who were assigned to read parts for Act III do so during these class periods. Continue the oral reading evaluations if you have not yet given everyone in the class a grade for oral reading.

LESSON TWELVE

Objectives
1. To review the main events and ideas presented in Act III
2. To assign the speaking parts for Act IV
3. To do the prereading work for Act IV

Activity #1
Give students a few minutes to formulate answers for the study guide questions for Act III, and then discuss the answers to the questions in detail. Write the answers on the board or overhead transparency so students can have the correct answers for study purposes.

Activity #2
Assign the following speaking parts for Act IV. (Tell students that they will be reading Act IV during the next class period.)

King	Queen
Hamlet	Rosencrantz
Guildenstern	Fortinbras
Horatio	Ophelia
Gentlemen	Laertes
Narrator	

Misc. Parts (Capt., Danes, Servant, Sailor, Messenger)

Activity #3
Prior to reading Act IV, students should preview the study questions and do the prereading vocabulary work for Act IV. Give students the remainder of this class period to do the prereading work and, if they finish that, to begin practicing their oral reading parts.

LESSON THIRTEEN

Objectives
1. To read Act IV of *Hamlet*
2. To evaluate students' oral reading

Activity
Have students who were assigned to read parts for Act IV do so during these class periods. Continue the oral reading evaluations if you have not yet given everyone in the class a grade for oral reading.

LESSON FOURTEEN

Objectives
    1. To review the main events and ideas presented in Act IV
    2. To assign the speaking parts for Act V
    3. To do the prereading work for Act V

Activity #1
    Give students a few minutes to formulate answers for the study guide questions for Act IV, and then discuss the answers to the questions in detail. Write the answers on the board or overhead transparency so students can have the correct answers for study purposes.

Activity #2
    Assign the following speaking parts for Act V. (Tell students that they will be reading Act V during the next class period.)

Clown 1	Clown 2
Hamlet	Horatio
Laertes	King
Queen	Osric
Narrator	Misc. Parts (Priest, Lord, Ambassador, Fortinbras)

Activity #3
    Prior to reading Act V, students should preview the study questions and do the prereading vocabulary work for Act V. Give students the remainder of this class period to do the prereading work and, if they finish that, to begin practicing their oral reading parts.

LESSON FIFTEEN

Objectives
    1. To read Act V of *Hamlet*
    2. To evaluate students' oral reading

Activity
    Have students who were assigned to read parts for Act V do so during these class periods. Continue the oral reading evaluations if you have not yet given everyone in the class a grade for oral reading.

LESSON SIXTEEN

Objectives
    1. To review the main ideas and events from Act V
    2. To review all of the vocabulary work done in this unit

Activity #1
    Give students a few minutes to formulate answers for the study guide questions for Act V, and then discuss the answers to the questions in detail.

Activity #2
    Choose one (or more) of the vocabulary review activities listed on the next page and spend your class period as directed in the activity. Some of the materials for these review activities are located in the Extra Activities Packet in this unit.

LESSON SEVENTEEN

Objectives
    1. To give students the opportunity to practice writing to persuade
    2. To give the teacher a chance to evaluate students' individual writing
    3. To give students the opportunity to correct their writing errors and produce an error-free paper

Activity
    Distribute Writing Assignment 2. Discuss the directions in detail and give students ample time to complete the assignment.

    While students are doing their writing assignments, call individuals to your desk (or some other private area) to discuss their papers from Writing Assignment 1. A Writing Evaluation Form is included with this unit to help structure your conferences.

VOCABULARY REVIEW ACTIVITIES

1. Divide your class into two teams and have an old-fashioned spelling or definition bee.

2. Give each of your students (or students in groups of two, three or four) a *Hamlet* Vocabulary Word Search Puzzle. The person (group) to find all of the vocabulary words in the puzzle first wins.

3. Give students a *Hamlet* Vocabulary Word Search Puzzle without the word list. The person or group to find the most vocabulary words in the puzzle wins.

4. Use a *Hamlet* Vocabulary Crossword Puzzle. Put the puzzle onto a transparency on the overhead projector (so everyone can see it), and do the puzzle together as a class.

5. Give students a *Hamlet* Vocabulary Matching Worksheet to do.

6. Divide your class into two teams. Use the *Hamlet* vocabulary words with their letters jumbled as a word list. Student 1 from Team A faces off against Student 1 from Team B. You write the first jumbled word on the board. The first student (1A or 1B) to unscramble the word wins the chance for his/her team to score points. If 1A wins the jumble, go to student 2A and give him/her a definition. He/she must give you the correct spelling of the vocabulary word which fits that definition. If he/she does, Team A scores a point, and you give student 3A a definition for which you expect a correctly spelled matching vocabulary word. Continue giving Team A definitions until some team member makes an incorrect response. An incorrect response sends the game back to the jumbled-word face off, this time with students 2A and 2B. Instead of repeating giving definitions to the first few students of each team, continue with the student after the one who gave the last incorrect response on the team. For example, if Team B wins the jumbled-word face-off, and student 5B gave the last incorrect answer for Team B, you would start this round of definition questions with student 6B, and so on. The team with the most points wins!

7. Have students write a story in which they correctly use as many vocabulary words as possible. Have students read their compositions orally! Post the most original compositions on your bulletin board.

WRITING ASSIGNMENT #2 - *Hamlet*

PROMPT

You belong to an advertising agency that has just been hired by Time Travel, Inc., a travel agency that offers time-travel tours to various places and events in the past and future. You have been hired to create the advertising brochure that will entice people to take the tour to London, England in 1601 to see a production of Shakespeare's play *Hamlet*. This brochure is to convince people to take the tour and to call for information regarding prices and schedules.

PREWRITING

Have you ever planned a vacation with your family? Maybe you have seen some of those fantastic brochures from the Disney theme parks or other places your family might have been going. They grab your attention, show you and tell you all about the best things they have to offer, and make you practically die with anticipation until you can get there.

You have had some background about Shakespeare, *Hamlet*, and life in the 1600s. Use parts of that information to create your brochure. Remember your audience will probably be mostly English and history teachers who have an interest in either Shakespeare or the 1600 time period--plus some people who just like to travel. What will entice them to take this tour as opposed to some other?

Make a list of reasons why people would want to go to Shakespeare's time. Make another list of reasons why people would want to go see *Hamlet*. Be creative; think of things your tour could include that would be of interest to these groups of people. Focus part of your brochure on the play *Hamlet*. Give a short synopsis of the play, and some background information.

Consider all of your notes and lists. How can you most effectively make a brochure with all of this information on it? Decide what information you want to include. Decide on what size your brochure will be (how large the pages will be and how many pages you will include).

DRAFTING

Sketch out a couple of different format/design ideas and pick the one you like best.

On regular notebook paper, write rough drafts for each of the little articles your brochure will include. You may use appropriate pictures or drawings in your brochure, too. Your final draft should look as professionally done as possible.

PROMPT

When you finish the rough draft of your paper, ask a student who sits near you to read it. After reading your rough draft, he/she should tell you what he/she liked best about your work, which parts were difficult to understand, and ways in which your work could be improved. Reread your paper considering your critic's comments, and make the corrections you think are necessary.

PROOFREADING

Do a final proofreading of your paper double-checking your grammar, spelling, organization, and the clarity of your ideas.

WRITING EVALUATION FORM - *Hamlet*

Name _____ Date _____

      Grade _____

Circle One For Each Item:

Grammar:	correct	errors noted on paper
Spelling:	correct	errors noted on paper
Punctuation:	correct	errors noted on paper
Legibility:	excellent	good fair poor

Strengths:

Weaknesses:

Comments/Suggestions:

LESSONS EIGHTEEN AND NINETEEN

Objectives
1. To study the characters of the play more closely
2. To give students the opportunity to practice their personal interaction skills in a small group setting.
3. To give students the opportunity to practice their public speaking skills as they report their small group findings.

Activity #1

Divide the class into six groups. Each group should be assigned one of the following characters (or group of characters):

Hamlet
King
Queen
Polonius
Laertes and Ophelia
Horatio and Fortinbras

Each group should look at its character(s) through the entire play. Group members should identify their character(s) role in the play, give a list of important characteristics of that character, and give at least one example (from the text) which shows each characteristic. (For example, if they list 4 characteristics, they should have 4 examples, one for each characteristic.) The group should also report any significant character changes its character develops through the play.

Groups may subdivide, assigning one act per student to break down the work load. If they do subdivide, each student should take his own notes, and when all students are done, they should discuss and compile their information.

One group member should be designated "secretary" to jot down the group's ideas. Another should be designated "spokesperson" to report the group's ideas to the class.

Activity #2   The groups will each report their findings and conclusions to the whole class. The teacher or a student should write down on the board or overhead all of the findings and conclusions. Students should all take notes from the board for later study.

LESSON TWENTY

Objectives
    1. To discuss *Hamlet* on interpretive and critical levels
    2. To take a closer look at Shakespeare's language and significant quotations from *Hamlet*

Activity

    Choose the questions from the Extra Discussion Questions/Writing Assignments which seem most appropriate for your students. A class discussion of these questions is most effective if students have been given the opportunity to formulate answers to the questions prior to the discussion. To this end, you may either have all the students formulate answers to all the questions, divide your class into groups and assign one or more questions to each group, or you could assign one question to each student in your class. The option you choose will make a difference in the amount of class time needed for this activity.

    After students have had ample time to formulate answers to the questions, begin your class discussion of the questions and the ideas presented by the questions. Be sure students take notes during the discussion so they have information to study for the unit test.

EXTRA WRITING ASSIGNMENTS/DISCUSSION QUESTIONS - *Hamlet*

Interpretation

1. What is the setting of *Hamlet*?

2. Where is the climax of the play? Explain your choice.

3. What are the main conflicts in the play, and how are they resolved?

4. Give a summary of the events in the plot.

Critical

5. Think of a different title for the play. Explain your choice.

6. Explain why *Hamlet* is a tragedy.

7. Describe the relationship between Hamlet and his mother.

8. What things motivate Hamlet?

9. Choose a passage from *Hamlet* (at least 10 lines). Analyze the meter, rhymes and word choice in relationship to the meaning and action of the passage.

10. Characterize William Shakespeare's style of writing. How does it contribute to the value of the play?

11. Compare and contrast Hamlet and Horatio.

12. Compare and contrast Horatio and Laertes.

13. There are several "bad guys" in *Hamlet*. Who do you think is the worst? Why?

14. Describe Hamlet's relationship with Ophelia.

15. What happened to Ophelia? Why?

16. Could the play *Hamlet* have been resolved without killing off all of the main characters? If so, how? If not, why not?

Hamlet Extra Discussion Questions page 2

17. Are the characters in *Hamlet* stereotypes? If so, explain why William Shakespeare used stereotypes. If not, explain how the characters merit individuality.

18. Explain the role of each: Rosencrantz & Guildenstern, Polonius, Osric, and Laertes.

Critical/Personal Response

19. Which minor character is the most important to the play?

20. What was Hamlet's biggest problem?

21. What would you have done if you were Hamlet and found out that your father had been murdered by your uncle and your mother?

22. Do you think the relationship between the King and Queen is realistic? Explain why or why not.

23. Who is responsible for Ophelia's death?

Personal Response

24. Did you enjoy reading *Hamlet*? Why or why not?

25. Suppose Hamlet had killed the King instead of Polonius at first. How would the play have changed?

26. Suppose Ophelia had lived. How would that have affected the story?

27. Would you have liked living in Hamlet's time of knights and castles? Why or why not?

28. Describe what your castle would be like if you were to build one.

29. Many writers today leave their endings open for a sequel (in case it becomes a box-office hit). Such is not the case with *Hamlet*. The end is definitely the end; all the main characters die. Which type of ending do you prefer? Why?

Hamlet Extra Discussion Questions page 3

Quotations
IDENTIFY AND EXPLAIN THE FOLLOWING QUOTATIONS FROM *Hamlet*.

1. A little more than kin and less than kind. (I.ii,64)

2. Seems, madam! Nay, it is. I know not "seems." (I.ii,76)

3. How weary, stale, flat, and unprofitable
   Seem to me all the uses of this world! (I.ii,133-134)

4. Frailty, thy name is woman! (I.ii,146)

5. Thrift, thrift, Horatio! The funeral baked meats
   Did coldly furnish forth the marriage tables. (I.ii,179-180)

6. Neither a borrower nor a lender be,
   For loan oft loses both itself and friend
   And borrowing dulls the edge of husbandry.
   This above all: To thine own self be true,
   And it must follow, as the night the day,
   Thou canst not then be false to any man. (I.iii,75-80)

7. Something is rotten in the state of Denmark. (I.iv,89)

8. Revenge his foul and most unnatural murder. (I.v,24)

9. My uncle!
   Aye, that incestuous, that adulterate beast (I.v,40-41)

10. Taint not thy mind, nor let thy soul contrive
    Against thy mother aught. Leave her to Heaven
    And to those thorns that in her bosom lodge
    To prick and sting her. (I.v,85-88)

11. The time is out of joint. Oh, cursed spite
    That ever I was born to set it right! (I.v,189-190)

Hamlet Extra Discussion Questions page 4

12. What majesty should be, what duty is,
    Why day is day, night night, and time is time,
    Were nothing but to waste night, day, and time.
    Therefore, since brevity is the soul of wit
    And tediousness the limbs and outward flourishes,
    I will be brief. (II.ii,87-92)

13. Though this be madness, yet there is method in't. (II.ii,207)

14. Why, then 'tis none to you, for there is nothing either good or bad but thinking makes it so. (II.ii,255-256)

15. What a piece of work is a man!
    How noble in reason! How infinite in faculty! In form and moving how express and admirable! In action how like an angel! In apprehension how like a god! The beauty of the world! The paragon of animals! And yet, to me, what is this quintessence of dust? Man delights not me -- no, nor woman neither, though by your smiling you seem to say so. (II.ii,315-321)

16. The play's the thing
    Wherein I'll catch the conscience of the King. (II.ii,633-634)

17. Madness in great ones must not unwatched go. (III.i,196)

18. Suit the action to the word, the word to the action, with this special observance, that you o'erstep not the modesty of nature. (III.ii,19-21)

19. The lady doth protest too much, methinks. (III.ii,240)

20. O good Horatio, I'll take the ghost's word for a thousand pound. Didst perceive? (III.ii,297-298)

21. O heart, lose not thy nature, let not ever
    The soul of Nero enter this firm bosom.
    Let me be cruel, not unnatural.
    I will speak daggers to her, but use none. (III.ii,411-413)

Hamlet Extra Discussion Questions page 5

22. My words fly up, my thoughts remain below.
    Words without thoughts never to Heaven go. (III.iii,97-98)

23. Oh, shame! Where is thy blush? (III.iv,82)

24. O Hamlet, speak no more.
    Thou turn'st mine eyes into my very soul,
    And there I see such black and grained spots
    As will not leave their tinct. (III.iv,88-91)

25. I must be cruel only to be kind. (III.iv.178)

26. What is a man
    If his chief good and market of his time
    Be but to sleep and feed? A beast, no more. (IV.iv,33-35)

27. Oh, from this time forth,
    My thoughts be bloody or be nothing worth. (IV.iv,65-66)

28. Alas, poor Yorick! I knew him, Horatio (V. i,202-203)

29. Sweets to the sweet. (V.i,266)

30. The cat will mew and dog will have his day. (V.i,315)

31. I am justly killed with mine own treachery. (V.ii,318)

32. The drink, the drink! I am poisoned. (V.ii,321)

33. The King, the King's to blame. (V.ii,331)

LESSON TWENTY-ONE

Objectives
1. To give students the opportunity to express their personal opinions
2. To extend students' knowledge of the characters and events in *Hamlet*
3. To give the teacher a chance to evaluate students' individual writing

Activity

Distribute Writing Assignment #3. Discuss the directions orally in detail. Allow the remaining class time for students to complete the activity.

If students do not have enough class time to finish, the papers may be collected at the beginning of the next class period.

Follow-Up: Follow up as in Writing Assignment 1, allowing students to correct their errors and turn in the revision for credit. A good time for your next writing conferences would be the day following the unit test.

WRITING ASSIGNMENT #3 - *Hamlet*

PROMPT

Hamlet certainly was thrown into a mess all of a sudden, wasn't he? Just put yourself in his shoes for a minute. Suppose your father died and your mother married your uncle practically before your father was cold in his coffin. Then, your father's ghost appeared to you telling you that he was murdered by your uncle (and mother) and asking you to get revenge for him. Whew! What in the world would you do? We all know what Hamlet's solution was and how it turned out. Your assignment is to write a composition in which you tell what you would have done if you were Hamlet, and how and why you would have done it.

PREWRITING

Your composition will be based on the fact that you believe the ghost or are at least sufficiently motivated by it to take some action. Think about what you would do. Jot down some notes. Would you create a plan for revenge? If so, what would it be? Remember, you are Hamlet, and you must use the characters presented in the play in your plans.

DRAFTING

Write an introductory paragraph in which you introduce the idea that you have seen your father's ghost and are motivated to take some action as per the ghost's request.

In the body of your composition, explain what plan of action you plan to take.

As the last paragraph of your composition write a paragraph telling how you think your plan will work, what may go wrong, and/or what unintended effects your plan may have on others.

PROMPT

When you finish the rough draft of your paper, ask a student who sits near you to read it. After reading your rough draft, he/she should tell you what he/she liked best about your work, which parts were difficult to understand, and ways in which your work could be improved. Reread your paper considering your critic's comments, and make the corrections you think are necessary.

PROOFREADING

Do a final proofreading of your paper double-checking your grammar, spelling, organization, and the clarity of your ideas.

LESSON TWENTY-TWO

Objectives
To give students some ways to cope with stressful situations in their own lives

NOTE: It is sad to note that so many young people have such stressful lives. Just growing up isn't easy even in the best of times, and today kids have to deal with violence in schools and their communities, drug and alcohol abuse, divorce, child or spouse abuse, AIDS, and who-knows-what-else. Teachers and social workers across the country talk about case after case after case in which students are just stressed-out.

This unit about *Hamlet* is a good time to talk about stress and ways to deal with it. Hamlet's life was certainly full of stress, and we saw what happened to him and those around him. Poor Ophelia, too. She didn't hold up very well, either. With these kinds of examples as springboards, this is an ideal time to bring in a guest speaker to talk with your students about ways to cope with a stressful life.

Your school probably is associated with several social workers who are or know people who are qualified to discuss this topic with your students. Invite one to your class.

Activity
Use this class period to have a guest speaker come in and discuss ways students can cope with stress in their lives.

IDEA: In preparation for this activity, you may wish to use an alternative Writing Assignment #3 in which students would write a composition in which they reveal the stresses they feel in their own lives.

LESSON TWENTY-THREE

Objective
To review the main ideas presented in *Hamlet*

Activity #1
Choose one of the review games/activities included in the packet and spend your class period as outlined there. Some materials for these activities are located in the Extra Activities Packet section of this unit.

Activity #2
Remind students that the Unit Test will be in the next class meeting. Stress the review of the Study Guides and their class notes as a last minute, brush-up review for homework.

REVIEW GAMES/ACTIVITIES - *Hamlet*

1. Ask the class to make up a unit test for Hamlet. The test should have 4 sections: matching, true/false, short answer, and essay. Students may use 1/2 period to make the test and then swap papers and use the other 1/2 class period to take a test a classmate has devised. (open book) You may want to use the unit test included in this packet or take questions from the students' unit tests to formulate your own test.

2. Take 1/2 period for students to make up true and false questions (including the answers). Collect the papers and divide the class into two teams. Draw a big tic-tac-toe board on the chalk board. Make one team X and one team O. Ask questions to each side, giving each student one turn. If the question is answered correctly, that students' team's letter (X or O) is placed in the box. If the answer is incorrect, no mark is placed in the box. The object is to get three marks in a row like tic-tac-toe. You may want to keep track of the number of games won for each team.

3. Take 1/2 period for students to make up questions (true/false and short answer). Collect the questions. Divide the class into two teams. You'll alternate asking questions to individual members of teams A & B (like in a spelling bee). The question keeps going from A to B until it is correctly answered, then a new question is asked. A correct answer does not allow the team to get another question. Correct answers are +2 points; incorrect answers are -1 point.

4. Have students pair up and quiz each other from their study guides and class notes.

5. Give students a *Hamlet* crossword puzzle to complete.

6. Divide your class into two teams. Use the *Hamlet* crossword words with their letters jumbled as a word list. Student 1 from Team A faces off against Student 1 from Team B. You write the first jumbled word on the board. The first student (1A or 1B) to unscramble the word wins the chance for his/her team to score points. If 1A wins the jumble, go to student 2A and give him/her a clue. He/she must give you the correct word which matches that clue. If he/she does, Team A scores a point, and you give student 3A a clue for which you expect another correct response. Continue giving Team A clues until some team member makes an incorrect response. An incorrect response sends the game back to the jumbled-word face off, this time with students 2A and 2B. Instead of repeating giving clues to the first few students of each team, continue with the student after the one who gave the last incorrect response on the team. For example, if Team B wins the jumbled-word face-off, and student 5B gave the last incorrect answer for Team B, you would start this round of clue questions with student 6B, and so on. The team with the most points wins!

UNIT TESTS

SHORT ANSWER UNIT TEST 1 - *Hamlet*

I. Matching/Identify

____ 1. Hamlet   A. Student and loyal friend of Hamlet

____ 2. Claudius   B. Polonius sends him to Paris to report on Laertes' conduct

____ 3. Gertrude   C. Prince of Norway, has lost his father

____ 4. Polonius   D. Prince of Denmark, has lost his father, his uncle is King

____ 5. Horatio   E. Daughter of Polonius

____ 6. Laertes   F. Umpired the fencing match between Hamlet and Laertes

____ 7. Ophelia   G. Hamlet's uncle

____ 8. Rosencrantz & Guildenstern   H. Ophelia's brother

____ 9. Osric   I. Hamlet's mother

____ 10. Fortinbras   J. Lord Chamberlain and chief counselor to Claudius

____ 11. Reynaldo   K. Came to Elsinore to help the King find out what Hamlet's trouble was

II. Short Answer

1. Hamlet is upset for two reasons. What are they?

2. Hamlet swears Horatio to two things. What are they?

3. Why does Polonius think Hamlet is "mad"?

Hamlet Short Answer Unit Test 1 Page 2

4. What arrangement does Hamlet make with Player 1?

5. Hamlet's famous "To be or not to be" soliloquy is in scene one. In a sentence or two paraphrase his main points.

6. What was the King's reaction to the play, and what did Hamlet and Horatio decide his reaction meant?

7. Why doesn't Hamlet kill the King when the King is kneeling?

8. How does Polonius die?

9. What is the content of the letters the King sends with Rosencrantz and Guildenstern to England with Hamlet?

10. What plan do the King and Laertes discuss to kill Hamlet?

11. Why does Hamlet jump into Ophelia's grave?

12. What did Hamlet do to Rosencrantz and Guildenstern?

Hamlet Short Answer Unit Test 1 Page 3

III. Quotations - Explain the significance of each of the following quotations:

1. This above all: To thine own self be true,
   And it must follow, as the night the day,
   Thou canst not then be false to any man. (I.iii,75-80)

2. My uncle!
   Aye, that incestuous, that adulterate beast (I.v,40-41)

3. Taint not thy mind, nor let thy soul contrive
   Against thy mother aught. Leave her to Heaven
   And to those thorns that in her bosom lodge
   To prick and sting her. (I.v,85-88)

4. The time is out of joint. Oh, cursed spite
   That ever I was born to set it right! (I.v,189-190)

5. Though this be madness, yet there is method in't. (II.ii,207)

Hamlet Short Answer Unit Test 1 Page 4

6. The play's the thing
   Wherein I'll catch the conscience of the King. (II.ii,633-634)

7. The lady doth protest too much, methinks. (III.ii,240)

8. I must be cruel only to be kind. (III.iv.178)

9. The cat will mew and dog will have his day. (V.i,315)

10. The King, the King's to blame. (V.ii,331)

Hamlet Short Answer Unit Test 1 Page 5

IV. Vocabulary

Listen to the vocabulary word and spell it. After you have spelled all the words, go back and write down the definition.

1.

2.

3.

4.

5.

6.

7.

8.

9.

10.

KEY: SHORT ANSWER UNIT TEST #1 - *Hamlet*

I. Matching/Identify

   D   1. Hamlet   A. Student and loyal friend of Hamlet

   G   2. Claudius   B. Polonius sends him to Paris to report on Laertes' conduct

   I   3. Gertrude   C. Prince of Norway, has lost his father

   J   4. Polonius   D. Prince of Denmark, has lost his father, his uncle is King

   A   5. Horatio   E. Daughter of Polonius

   H   6. Laertes   F. Umpired the fencing match between Hamlet and Laertes

   E   7. Ophelia   G. Hamlet's uncle

   K   8. Rosencrantz &   H. Ophelia's brother
             Guildenstern

   F   9. Osric   I. Hamlet's mother

   C   10. Fortinbras   J. Lord Chamberlain and chief counselor to Claudius

   B   11. Reynaldo   K. Came to Elsinore to help the King find out what Hamlet's trouble was

II. Short Answer

1. Hamlet is upset for two reasons. What are they?
    His father has died, and his uncle has married his mother less than two months after his father's death. It was not a respectable period of time to wait, besides which the marriage in Hamlet's time was considered incestuous.

2. Hamlet swears Horatio to two things. What are they?
    He swears him to secrecy about the events of this evening (seeing the ghost) and to go along with him should he pretend to be crazy.

3. Why does Polonius think Hamlet is "mad"?
    He thinks Ophelia's rejections have been too much for Hamlet, that Hamlet is love-sick.

4. What arrangement does Hamlet make with Player 1?

    He arranges to have several of his own lines put into the play (to make the action of the play as closely related to the actual events of his father's murder as possible).

5. Hamlet's famous "To be or not to be" soliloquy is in scene one. In a sentence or two paraphrase his main points.

    He is pondering whether a miserable life is better than the unknown of death.

6. What was the King's reaction to the play, and what did Hamlet and Horatio decide his reaction meant?

    The King got up and called for the lights. Hamlet and Horatio were convinced that the ghost was right, that Claudius had murdered King Hamlet.

7. Why doesn't Hamlet kill the King when the King is kneeling?

    Hamlet wants the King to die without a chance for a last confession, as his father died. He thinks if the King is praying, he may not be in sin enough to get eternal punishment.

8. How does Polonius die?

    Polonius is in the Queen's room while she and Hamlet are talking. He hides behind the tapestry but makes some noise. Hamlet runs through the tapestry with his sword (actually thinking Claudius might be there), killing Polonius.

9. What is the content of the letters the King sends with Rosencrantz and Guildenstern to England with Hamlet?

    The King wants Hamlet to be killed as soon as he reaches England.

10. What plan do the King and Laertes discuss to kill Hamlet?

    They plan to set up a duel between Laertes and Hamlet in which Laertes will honorably kill Hamlet, or if Hamlet lives, the King will poison him.

11. Why does Hamlet jump into Ophelia's grave?

    He shows that his sorrow is as great as Laertes'.

12. What did Hamlet do to Rosencrantz and Guildenstern?

    Hamlet replaced their letters (which called for Hamlet's execution) with letters which called for the execution of Rosencrantz and Guildenstern.

III. Quotations

   Student responses for quotations will depend upon your interpretation presented in class.

IV. Vocabulary - Choose ten words from the vocabulary lists. Read them orally so your students can write them down for part IV of the test.

SHORT ANSWER UNIT TEST 2 - *Hamlet*

I. Matching

____ 1. Hamlet   A. Lord Chamberlain and chief counselor to Claudius

____ 2. Claudius   B. Umpired the fencing match between Hamlet and Laertes

____ 3. Gertrude   C. Ophelia's brother

____ 4. Polonius   D. Came to Elsinore to help the king find out what Hamlet's trouble was

____ 5. Horatio   E. Student and loyal friend of Hamlet

____ 6. Laertes   F. Polonius sends him to Paris to report on Laertes' conduct

____ 7. Ophelia   G. Hamlet's mother

____ 8. Rosencrantz & Guildenstern   H. Prince of Norway, has lost his father

____ 9. Osric   I. Hamlet's uncle

____ 10. Fortinbras   J. Daughter of Polonius

____ 11. Reynaldo   K. Prince of Denmark, has lost his father, his uncle is King

II. Short Answer

1. What is Polonius' plan for testing his theory that Hamlet is love-crazy?

2. Rosencrantz and Guildenstern finally meet with Hamlet, and Hamlet discovers they were sent for by the King. How does Hamlet describe his personal problems to them? What does he tell them?

3. What arrangement does Hamlet make with Player 1?

Hamlet Short Answer Unit Test 2 Page 2

4. What do the King and Polonius decide about Hamlet's condition after eavesdropping on Hamlet and Ophelia?

5 The King has Rosencrantz and Guildenstern prepare to do what? Why?

6. Why doesn't Hamlet kill the King when the King is kneeling?

7. How does Polonius die?

8. Why must the King "not put the strong arm on" Hamlet?

9. What plan do the King and Laertes discuss to kill Hamlet?

10. What did Hamlet do to Rosencrantz and Guildenstern?

11. What happens to the King, Hamlet, Laertes, and the Queen?

Hamlet Short Answer Unit Test 2 Page 3
III. Quotations
　　　Explain the significance of the following quotations:

1. How weary, stale, flat, and unprofitable
　Seem to me all the uses of this world! (I.ii,133-134)

2. Thrift, thrift, Horatio! The funeral baked meats
　Did coldly furnish forth the marriage tables. (I.ii,179-180)

3. Revenge his foul and most unnatural murder. (I.v,24)

4. The time is out of joint. Oh, cursed spite
　That ever I was born to set it right! (I.v,189-190)

5. Why, then 'tis none to you, for there is nothing either good or bad but thinking makes it so. (II.ii,255-256)

Hamlet Short Answer Unit Test 2 Page 4

6. What a piece of work is a man!
How noble in reason! How infinite in faculty! In form and moving how express and admirable! In action how like an angel! In apprehension how like a god! The beauty of the world! The paragon of animals! And yet, to me, what is this quintessence of dust? Man delights not me -- no, nor woman neither, though by your smiling you seem to say so. (II.ii,315-321)

7. O good Horatio, I'll take the ghost's word for a thousand pound. Didst perceive? (III.ii,297-298)

8. O heart, lose not thy nature, let not ever
The soul of Nero enter this firm bosom.
Let me be cruel, not unnatural.
I will speak daggers to her, but use none. (III.ii,411-413)

9.   Oh, from this time forth,
My thoughts be bloody or be nothing worth. (IV.iv,65-66)

10. I am justly killed with mine own treachery. (V.ii,318)

11. The drink, the drink! I am poisoned. (V.ii,321)

Hamlet Short Answer Unit Test 2 Page 5

IV. Vocabulary

    Listen to the vocabulary word and spell it. After you have spelled all the words, go back and write down the definition.

1.

2.

3.

4.

5.

6.

7.

8.

9.

10.

KEY: SHORT ANSWER UNIT TEST 2 *Hamlet*

I. Matching (Use this matching key also for the Advanced Short Answer Unit Test)

__K__ 1. Hamlet A. Lord Chamberlain and chief counselor to Claudius

__I__ 2. Claudius B. Umpired the fencing match between Hamlet and Laertes

__G__ 3. Gertrude C. Ophelia's brother

__A__ 4. Polonius D. Came to Elsinore to help the King find out what Hamlet's trouble was

__E__ 5. Horatio E. Student and loyal friend of Hamlet

__C__ 6. Laertes F. Polonius sends him to Paris to report on Laertes' conduct

__J__ 7. Ophelia G. Hamlet's mother

__D__ 8. Rosencrantz & Guildenstern H. Prince of Norway, has lost his father

__B__ 9. Osric I. Hamlet's uncle

__H__ 10. Fortinbras J. Daughter of Polonius

__F__ 11. Reynaldo K. Prince of Denmark, has lost his father, his uncle is King

II. Short Answer

1. What is Polonius' plan for testing his theory that Hamlet is love-crazy?
    He wants to have Hamlet meet Ophelia. He (Polonius) will hide and eavesdrop on the conversation to determine whether or not Hamlet is love-sick.

2. Rosencrantz and Guildenstern finally meet with Hamlet, and Hamlet discovers they were sent for by the King. How does Hamlet describe his personal problems to them? What does he tell them?
    Hamlet basically says that he thought the world was wonderful and man was the most wonderful part of the world, but now he finds that things are not wonderful. He finds no delight in man or woman.

3. What arrangement does Hamlet make with Player 1?
    He arranges to have several of his own lines put into the play (to make the action of the play as closely related to the actual events of his father's murder as possible).

4. What do the King and Polonius decide about Hamlet's condition after eavesdropping on Hamlet and Ophelia?
    They decide he is not love-sick; rather, he has some other trouble deep in his soul.

5. The King has Rosencrantz and Guildenstern prepare to do what? Why?
    He has them prepare to take Hamlet to England. Claudius is beginning to feel threatened by Hamlet, and he wants him away from Elsinore. In fact, he wants Hamlet dead.

6. Why doesn't Hamlet kill the King when the King is kneeling?
    Hamlet wants the King to die without a chance for a last confession, as his father died. He thinks if the King is praying, he may not be in sin enough to get eternal punishment.

7. How does Polonius die?
    Polonius is in the Queen's room while she and Hamlet are talking. He hides behind the tapestry but makes some noise. Hamlet runs through the tapestry with his sword (actually thinking Claudius might be there), killing Polonius.

8. Why must the King "not put the strong arm on" Hamlet?
    Hamlet's mother truly loves him and would want no harm to come to him, and the people of Denmark love him and would be uneasy if something would happen to him.

9. What plan do the King and Laertes discuss to kill Hamlet?
    They plan to set up a duel between Laertes and Hamlet in which Laertes will honorably kill Hamlet, or if Hamlet lives, the King will poison him.

10. What did Hamlet do to Rosencrantz and Guildenstern?
    Hamlet replaced their letters (which called for Hamlet's execution) with letters which called for the execution of Rosencrantz and Guildenstern.

11. What happens to the King, Hamlet, Laertes, and the Queen?
    The King is run through and killed by Hamlet. Hamlet is killed by the poison on Laertes's sword. Laertes is killed by the poison on his own sword. The Queen is poisoned and killed by the drink the King had prepared for Hamlet.

III. Quotations
    Student responses to the quotations will depend upon the interpretations given during discussions.

IV. Vocabulary - Choose ten of the vocabulary words to dictate for your students.

ADVANCED SHORT ANSWER UNIT TEST - *Hamlet*

I. Matching

____ 1. Hamlet   A. Lord Chamberlain and chief counselor to Claudius

____ 2. Claudius   B. Umpired the fencing match between Hamlet and Laertes

____ 3. Gertrude   C. Ophelia's brother

____ 4. Polonius   D. Came to Elsinore to help the King find out what Hamlet's trouble was

____ 5. Horatio   E. Student and loyal friend of Hamlet

____ 6. Laertes   F. Polonius sends him to Paris to report on Laertes' conduct

____ 7. Ophelia   G. Hamlet's mother

____ 8. Rosencrantz & Guildenstern   H. Prince of Norway, has lost his father

____ 9. Osric   I. Hamlet's uncle

____ 10. Fortinbras   J. Daughter of Polonius

____ 11. Reynaldo   K. Prince of Denmark, has lost his father, his uncle is King

II. Short Answer

1. Describe the relationship between Hamlet and his mother.

2. Compare and contrast Hamlet and Horatio.

Hamlet Advanced Short Answer Unit Test Page 2

3. Describe Hamlet's relationship with Ophelia.

4. Explain why *Hamlet* is a tragedy.

5. Explain what Hamlet's problem(s) is(are).

6. Who is the most important character in the play (besides Hamlet)? Defend your answer.

Hamlet Advanced Short Answer Unit Test Page 3

7. What is one theme in *Hamlet*? Give specific examples of it from the text.

8. What is the main conflict in *Hamlet*? Justify your answer.

9. Was Hamlet "mad"? Defend your answer.

10. Explain Ophelia's role in the play.

Hamlet Advanced Short Answer Unit Test Page 4

III. Quotations: Explain the significance of the following quotations:

1. A little more than kin and less than kind. (I.ii,64)

2. Seems, madam! Nay, it is. I know not "seems." (I.ii,76)

3. Frailty, thy name is woman! (I.ii,146)

4. Thrift, thrift, Horatio! The funeral baked meats
   Did coldly furnish forth the marriage tables. (I.ii,179-180)

5. This above all: To thine own self be true,
   And it must follow, as the night the day,
   Thou canst not then be false to any man. (I.iii,75-80)

6. The time is out of joint. Oh, cursed spite
   That ever I was born to set it right! (I.v,189-190)

7. What majesty should be, what duty is,
   Why day is day, night night, and time is time,
   Were nothing but to waste night, day, and time.
   Therefore, since brevity is the soul of wit
   And tediousness the limbs and outward flourishes,
   I will be brief. (II.ii,87-92)

Hamlet Advanced Short Answer Unit Test Page 5

8. What a piece of work is a man!
How noble in reason! How infinite in faculty! In form and moving how express and admirable! In action how like an angel! In apprehension how like a god! The beauty of the world! The paragon of animals! And yet, to me, what is this quintessence of dust? Man delights not me -- no, nor woman neither, though by your smiling you seem to say so. (II.ii,315-321)

9. The play's the thing
Wherein I'll catch the conscience of the King. (II.ii,633-634)

10. O good Horatio, I'll take the ghost's word for a thousand pound. Didst perceive? (III.ii,297-298)

11. Oh, shame! Where is thy blush? (III.iv,82)

12. I must be cruel only to be kind. (III.iv.178)

13. Sweets to the sweet. (V.i,266)

14. I am justly killed with mine own treachery. (V.ii,318)

15. The drink, the drink! I am poisoned. (V.ii,321)

16. The King, the King's to blame. (V.ii,331)

Hamlet Advanced Short Answer Unit Test Page 6

IV. Vocabulary

Listen to the vocabulary words and write them down. Go back later and write a composition in which you use all the words. The composition should relate in some way to *Hamlet*.

MULTIPLE CHOICE UNIT TEST 1- *Hamlet*

I. Matching

____ 1. Hamlet   A. Student and loyal friend of Hamlet

____ 2. Claudius   B. Polonius sends him to Paris to report on Laertes' conduct

____ 3. Gertrude   C. Prince of Norway, has lost his father

____ 4. Polonius   D. Prince of Denmark, has lost his father, his uncle is King

____ 5. Horatio   E. Daughter of Polonius

____ 6. Laertes   F. Umpired the fencing match between Hamlet and Laertes

____ 7. Ophelia   G. Hamlet's uncle

____ 8. Rosencrantz &   H. Ophelia's brother
        Guildenstern

____ 9. Osric   I. Hamlet's mother

____ 10. Fortinbras   J. Lord Chamberlain and chief counselor to Claudius

____ 11. Reynaldo   K. Came to Elsinore to help the King find out what Hamlet's trouble was

II. Multiple Choice

1. Hamlet is upset for two reasons. What are they?
    A. His mother has been ignoring him, and his fiancée has canceled the wedding plans.
    B. His father has died, and his uncle has declared war on Fortinbras.
    C. He wants to travel for about a year, but he is afraid to leave his mother, because she has been acting strangely since the King's death.
    D. His father has died, and his uncle has married his mother less than two months after his father's death.

2. What did the ghost tell Hamlet?
    A. The ghost told Hamlet that King Hamlet was murdered by Claudius, and it asked Hamlet to revenge the murder.
    B. The ghost told Hamlet that he was not really the son of King Hamlet. The Queen had lied, and Hamlet was really the son of Claudius.
    C. The ghost told Hamlet that Fortinbras is the rightful ruler, and asks Hamlet to help him gain the throne.
    D. The ghost tells Hamlet that he should take his mother and flee to Sweden.

Hamlet Multiple Choice Unit Test 1 Page 2

3. Hamlet swears Horatio to two things. What are they?
    A. Hamlet asks Horatio to promise to protect his mother, and to defend the country against Fortinbras.
    B. Hamlet asks Horatio to promise to attend Mass for him everyday for a year if he dies, and to marry Ophelia.
    B. Hamlet asks Horatio not to reveal the events of the evening, and to go along with him (Hamlet) if he pretends to be crazy.
    D. Hamlet asks Horatio to defend him in battle, and to kill Claudius if he (Hamlet) does not do it first.

4. Why have Rosencrantz and Guildenstern come to the castle?
    A. They have come to help the Queen redecorate in a manner suitable to Claudius.
    B. They have come to tutor Hamlet so that he can go on to the University in Paris or London.
    C. They are master soldiers who have come to prepare the troops for battle.
    D. They have come to find out why Hamlet is acting so strangely and to report their findings to the King.

5. What is Polonius' plan for testing his theory about Hamlet's madness?
    A. He wants to stage a duel and see if Hamlet is mentally aware enough to fight.
    B. He wants the most famous doctors to be brought from all over Europe to observe and study Hamlet, then to make a diagnosis and treatment plan.
    C. He wants to have Hamlet meet Ophelia. He (Polonius) will hide and eavesdrop on the conversation.
    D. He wants the priest to come from Rome to perform an exorcism on Hamlet.

6. Hamlet's famous "To be or not to be" soliloquy is in Scene One. Which of the following paraphrases his main points?
    A. He questions whether love, either romantic or family love, is worth all of the pain it causes.
    B. He is pondering whether a miserable life is better than the unknown of the death.
    C. He questions whether peace of mind is a good substitute for material wealth.
    D. He questions the traditions about succession to the throne in Denmark. He feels that either he or his mother should be the rightful successor to his dead father.

7. What do the King and Polonius decide about Hamlet's condition after eavesdropping on Hamlet and Ophelia?
    A. They decide he is love-sick, and the only cure is to find him another love.
    B. They decide he is not love-sick; rather; he has some other trouble deep in his soul.
    C. They decide his father's death has left him troubled.
    D. They decide he's not sick at all; he's just being a spoiled brat throwing a tantrum.

Hamlet Multiple Choice Unit Test 1 Page 3

8. What was the King's reaction to the play, and what did Hamlet and Horatio decide his reaction meant?
   A. The King had no reaction to the play. They decided it meant they were wrong, and that he was innocent after all.
   B. The King laughed and laughed. They decided he didn't really get the point, and they would have to be more direct the next time.
   C. The King got up and called for the lights. They were convinced that the ghost had been correct.
   D. The King clenched his teeth and gripped the arms of his chair, but said nothing. They thought they were on the right track, but would need to do something else to force the King into making a confession.

9. Why doesn't Hamlet kill the King when the King is kneeling?
   A. Hamlet wants his mother to be there to witness the deed.
   B. Hamlet loses heart, and realizes that his father would not have wanted another murder committed.
   C. Hamlet wants the King to die without a chance for a last confession. If he is praying, he may not be in enough sin to get eternal punishment.
   D. He thinks he hears noises in the hallway. He is afraid that someone will see him. He decides to wait until he can be sure they are alone.

10. How does Polonius die?
    A. He and Ophelia are standing on the top of the castle tower, talking. Ophelia becomes enraged and pushes him over the edge.
    B. Polonius is hiding in the Queen's room while she and Hamlet are talking. Hamlet runs through the tapestry, thinking it may be Claudius, and kills Polonius.
    C. The King decides to get rid of any potential enemies. He sends Rosencrantz and Guildenstern to murder Polonius. They make it look like a suicide.
    D. He realizes that Hamlet has been right all along. He kills himself in his grief and remorse.

11. What would Hamlet have his mother do?
    A. He wants her to go to England.
    B. He wants her to stop sleeping with the King.
    C. He wants her to have the marriage annulled by the Church.
    D. He wants her to poison the King at dinner the next night.

Hamlet Multiple Choice Unit Test 1 Page 4

12. What prompts Hamlet to say, "My thoughts be bloody or be nothing worth!"?
    A. He feels guilty for killing Polonius.
    B. He realizes that his father has been murdered, his uncle is a murderer, his mother is living in an incestuous marriage, and the soldiers he has just seen are going to kill each other over a little piece of land which is not worth anything.
    C. He decides to offer Rosencrantz and Guildenstern more money than the King is giving them, in the hopes that they will turn traitor on the King and murder him.
    D. He realizes that he has been thinking about death and destruction almost constantly. He feels sad, and wonders if he will ever again be able to think peaceful thoughts.

13. What plan do the King and Laertes discuss to kill Hamlet?
    A. They will go to see him, disguised as beggars. Then they will rob him and beat him to death.
    B. They plan to set up a duel between Laertes and Hamlet. Either Laertes will honorably kill Hamlet, or, if he survives, the King will poison him.
    C. They plan to go to him and escort him back to Denmark. On the way, they will stage a shipwreck. They will leave Hamlet in the water to perish, and they will be rescued by another ship.
    D. They plan to force Horatio to do it. If he refuses they will kill his family.

14. What does the King say to Laertes to console him after Laertes and Hamlet are separated?
    A. The King tells Laertes not to worry, that he (Laertes) will soon have the appropriate time and place to kill Hamlet.
    B. He offers Laertes money and a piece of land as consolation.
    C. He tells Laertes he will have the priest say a special prayer to make sure Ophelia's soul goes to heaven.
    D. He tells Laertes that he (the King) will exile Hamlet instead of killing him.

15. What does Hamlet do to Rosencrantz and Guildenstern?
    A. He pays a group of thugs to beat them and leave them for dead.
    B. He offers them money and reminds them that the three of them used to be friends. He asks them to stay with him.
    C. He arranged for them to be kidnaped and taken to Poland.
    D. He replaced their letters (which called for Hamlet's execution) with letters which called for their executions.

16-19. What happens to each of these characters?
    16. ___ The King   A. Drinks a poisoned beverage
    17. ___ Hamlet   B. Is run through with Hamlet's sword.
    18. ___ Laertes   C. Is killed by the poison on his opponent's sword
    19. ___ The Queen   D. Is killed by the poison on his own sword

Hamlet Multiple Choice Unit Test 1 Page 5

III. Quotations: Identify the speaker for each quotation by matching the letter by the character's name to the appropriate quotation.

    A=Hamlet   B=Queen   C=Ghost   D=King   E=Polonius
    F=Laertes   G=Marcellus   H=Horatio   I=Guildenstern   J=Ophelia

1. How weary, stale, flat, and unprofitable
   Seem to me all the uses of this world! (I.ii,133-134)

2. Neither a borrower nor a lender be,
   For loan oft loses both itself and friend
   And borrowing dulls the edge of husbandry.
   This above all: To thine own self be true,
   And it must follow, as the night the day,
   Thou canst not then be false to any man. (I.iii,75-80)

3. Something is rotten in the state of Denmark. (I.iv,89)

4. Revenge his foul and most unnatural murder. (I.v,24)

5. Taint not thy mind, nor let thy soul contrive
   Against thy mother aught. Leave her to Heaven
   And to those thorns that in her bosom lodge
   To prick and sting her. (I.v,85-88)

6. Though this be madness, yet there is method in't. (II.ii,207)

7. What a piece of work is a man!
   How noble in reason! How infinite in faculty! In form and moving how express and admirable! In action how like an angel! In apprehension how like a god! The beauty of the world! The paragon of animals! And yet, to me, what is this quintessence of dust? Man delights not me -- no, nor woman neither, though by your smiling you seem to say so. (II.ii,315-321)

8. The play's the thing
   Wherein I'll catch the conscience of the King. (II.ii,633-634)

9. The lady doth protest too much, methinks. (III.ii,240)

10. My words fly up, my thoughts remain below.
    Words without thoughts never to Heaven go. (III.iii,97-98)

Hamlet Multiple Choice Unit Test 1 Page 6
Quotations Continued

11. O Hamlet, speak no more.
    Thou turn'st mine eyes into my very soul,
    And there I see such black and grained spots
    As will not leave their tinct. (III.iv,88-91)

12. I must be cruel only to be kind. (III.iv.178)

13.   Oh, from this time forth,
    My thoughts be bloody or be nothing worth. (IV.iv,65-66)

14. Sweets to the sweet. (V.i,266)

15. I am justly killed with mine own treachery. (V.ii,318)

16. The drink, the drink! I am poisoned. (V.ii,321)

17. The King, the King's to blame. (V.ii,331)

Hamlet Multiple Choice Unit Test 1 Page 7

IV. Vocabulary

____ 1. CHURLISH		A. Tendons; muscles
____ 2. SUPERFLUOUS		B. Demanding or arousing pity
____ 3. ENTREAT		C. To address an earnest or urgent request to
____ 4. PERNICIOUS		D. The face or facial expression
____ 5. COMMINGLED		E. Difficult to work with
____ 6. PITEOUS		F. A reply to an answer; a rejoinder
____ 7. AMBIGUOUS		G. To make an earnest request of
____ 8. VOW		H. Exciting wonder and awe
____ 9. MALICIOUS		I. Reduction in amount, degree, or intensity
____ 10. APPURTENANCE		J. Mixed together
____ 11. ABATEMENTS		K. An earnest promise
____ 12. DISCORD		L. Being beyond what is required or sufficient
____ 13. REPLICATION		M. Tension or strife
____ 14. SINEWS		N. Spiteful
____ 15. PERDITION		O. Open to more than one interpretation
____ 16. DIVULGING		P. A means of inflicting severe suffering, vengeance or punishment
____ 17. VISAGE		Q. Deadly; destructive; wicked
____ 18. BESEECH		R. Loss of the soul; eternal damnation
____ 19. SCOURGE		S. Becoming known
____ 20. PORTENTOUS		T. Something added to another, more important thing; an appendage

MULTIPLE CHOICE UNIT TEST 2 - *Hamlet*

I. Matching

____ 1. Hamlet   A. Lord Chamberlain and chief counselor to Claudius

____ 2. Claudius   B. Umpired the fencing match between Hamlet and Laertes

____ 3. Gertrude   C. Ophelia's brother

____ 4. Polonius   D. Came to Elsinore to help the King find out what Hamlet's trouble was

____ 5. Horatio   E. Student and loyal friend of Hamlet

____ 6. Laertes   F. Polonius sends him to Paris to report on Laertes' conduct

____ 7. Ophelia   G. Hamlet's mother

____ 8. Rosencrantz & Guildenstern   H. Prince of Norway, has lost his father

____ 9. Osric   I. Hamlet's uncle

____ 10. Fortinbras   J. Daughter of Polonius

____ 11. Reynaldo   K. Prince of Denmark, has lost his father, his uncle is King

II. Multiple Choice

1. Hamlet is upset for two reasons. What are they?
    A. His father has died, and his uncle has married his mother less than two months after his father's death.
    B. His father has died, and his uncle has declared war on Fortinbras.
    C. He wants to travel for about a year, but he is afraid to leave his mother, because she has been acting strangely since the King's death.
    D. His mother has been ignoring him, and his fiancée has canceled the wedding plans.

2. What did the ghost tell Hamlet?
    A. The ghost told Hamlet that Fortinbras is the rightful ruler, and asks Hamlet to help him gain the throne.
    B. The ghost told Hamlet that he was not really the son of King Hamlet. The Queen had lied, and Hamlet was really the son of Claudius.
    C. The ghost told Hamlet that King Hamlet was murdered by Claudius, and it asked Hamlet to revenge the murder.
    D. The ghost tells Hamlet that he should take his mother and flee to Sweden.

Hamlet Multiple Choice Unit Test 2 Page 2

3. Hamlet swears Horatio to two things. What are they?
    A. Hamlet asks Horatio to promise to protect his mother, and to defend the country against Fortinbras.
    B. Hamlet asks Horatio not to reveal the events of the evening, and to go along with him (Hamlet) if he pretends to be crazy.
    C. Hamlet asks Horatio to promise to attend Mass for him everyday for a year if he dies, and to marry Ophelia.
    D. Hamlet asks Horatio to defend him in battle, and to kill Claudius if he (Hamlet) does not do it first.

4. Why have Rosencrantz and Guildenstern come to the castle?
    A. They have come to help the Queen redecorate in a manner suitable to Claudius.
    B. They have come to find out why Hamlet is acting so strangely and to report their findings to the King.
    C. They are master soldiers who have come to prepare the troops for battle.
    D. They have come to tutor Hamlet so that he can go on to the University in Paris or London.

5. What is Polonius' plan for testing his theory about Hamlet's madness?
    A. He wants to stage a duel and see if Hamlet is mentally aware enough to fight.
    B. He wants the most famous doctors to be brought from all over Europe to observe and study Hamlet, then to make a diagnosis and treatment plan.
    C. He wants to have Hamlet meet Ophelia. He (Polonius) will hide and eavesdrop on the conversation.
    D. He wants the priest to come from Rome to perform an exorcism on Hamlet.

6. Hamlet's famous "To be or not to be" soliloquy is in Scene One. Which of the following paraphrases his main points?
    A. He questions whether love, either romantic or family love, is worth all of the pain it causes.
    B. He is pondering whether a miserable life is better than the unknown of the death.
    C. He questions whether peace of mind is a good substitute for material wealth.
    D. He questions the traditions about succession to the throne in Denmark. He feels that either he or his mother should be the rightful successor to his dead father.

7. What do the King and Polonius decide about Hamlet's condition after eavesdropping on Hamlet and Ophelia?
    A. They decide he is love-sick, and the only cure is to find him another love.
    B. They decide he's not sick at all; he's just being a spoiled brat throwing a tantrum.
    C. They decide his father's death has left him troubled.
    D. They decide he is not love-sick; rather; he has some other trouble deep in his soul.

Hamlet Multiple Choice Unit Test 2 Page 3

8. What was the King's reaction to the play, and what did Hamlet and Horatio decide his reaction meant?
    A. The King got up and called for the lights. They were convinced that the ghost had been correct.
    B. The King laughed and laughed. They decided he didn't really get the point, and they would have to be more direct the next time.
    C. The King had no reaction to the play. They decided it meant they were wrong, and that he was innocent after all.
    D. The King clenched his teeth and gripped the arms of his chair, but said nothing. They thought they were on the right track, but would need to do something else to force the King into making a confession.

9. Why doesn't Hamlet kill the King when the King is kneeling?
    A. Hamlet wants his mother to be there to witness the deed.
    B. Hamlet loses heart, and realizes that his father would not have wanted another murder committed.
    C. He thinks he hears noises in the hallway. He is afraid that someone will see him. He decides to wait until he can be sure they are alone.
    D. Hamlet wants the King to die without a chance for a last confession. If he is praying, he may not be in enough sin to get eternal punishment.

10. How does Polonius die?
    A. He and Ophelia are standing on the top of the castle tower, talking. Ophelia becomes enraged and pushes him over the edge.
    B. The King decides to get rid of any potential enemies. He sends Rosencrantz and Guildenstern to murder Polonius. They make it look like a suicide.
    C. Polonius is hiding in the Queen's room while she and Hamlet are talking. Hamlet runs through the tapestry, thinking it may be Claudius, and kills Polonius.
    D. He realizes that Hamlet has been right all along. He kills himself in his grief and remorse.

11. What would Hamlet have his mother do?
    A. He wants her to stop sleeping with the King.
    B. He wants her to go to England.
    C. He wants her to have the marriage annulled by the Church.
    D. He wants her to poison the King at dinner the next night.

Hamlet Multiple Choice Unit Test 2 Page 4

12. What prompts Hamlet to say, "My thoughts be bloody or be nothing worth!"?
    A. He feels guilty for killing Polonius.
    B. He realizes that he has been thinking about death and destruction almost constantly. He feels sad, and wonders if he will ever again be able to think peaceful thoughts.
    C. He decides to offer Rosencrantz and Guildenstern more money than the King is giving them, in the hopes that they will turn traitor on the King and murder him for Hamlet.
    D. He realizes that his father has been murdered, his uncle is a murderer, his mother is living in an incestuous marriage, and the soldiers he has just seen are going to kill each other over a little piece of land which is not worth anything.

13. What plan do the King and Laertes discuss to kill Hamlet?
    A. They will go to see him, disguised as beggars. Then they will rob him and beat him to death.
    B. They plan to force Horatio to do it. If he refuses they will kill his family.
    C. They plan to go to him and escort him back to Denmark. On the way, they will stage a shipwreck. They will leave Hamlet in the water to perish, and they will be rescued by another ship.
    D. They plan to set up a duel between Laertes and Hamlet. Either Laertes will honorably kill Hamlet, or, if he survives, the King will poison him.

14. What does the King say to Laertes to console him after Laertes and Hamlet are separated?
    A. He tells Laertes he will have the priest say a special prayer to make sure Ophelia's soul goes to heaven.
    B. He offers Laertes money and a piece of land as consolation.
    C. The King tells Laertes not to worry, that he (Laertes) will soon have the appropriate time and place to kill Hamlet.
    D. He tells Laertes that he (the King) will exile Hamlet instead of killing him.

15. What does Hamlet do to Rosencrantz and Guildenstern?
    A. He replaced their letters (which called for Hamlet's execution) with letters which called for their executions.
    B. He offers them money and reminds them that the three of them used to be friends. He asks them to stay with him.
    C. He arranged for them to be kidnaped and taken to Poland.
    D. He pays a group of thugs to beat them and leave them for dead.

16-19. What happens to each of these characters?
    16. ___ The King   A. Is killed by the poison on his own sword
    17. ___ Hamlet   B. Is run through with Hamlet's sword.
    18. ___ Laertes   C. Drinks a poisoned beverage
    19. ___ The Queen   D. Is killed by the poison on his opponent's sword

Hamlet Multiple Choice Unit Test 2 Page 5

III. Quotations: Identify the speaker for each quotation by matching the letter by the character's name to the appropriate quotation.

    A=Horatio   B=Ophelia   C=King   D=Ghost   E=Marcellus
    F=Hamlet   G=Polonius   H= Laertes   I=Guildenstern   J=Queen

1. How weary, stale, flat, and unprofitable
   Seem to me all the uses of this world! (I.ii,133-134)

2. Neither a borrower nor a lender be,
   For loan oft loses both itself and friend
   And borrowing dulls the edge of husbandry.
   This above all: To thine own self be true,
   And it must follow, as the night the day,
   Thou canst not then be false to any man. (I.iii,75-80)

3. Something is rotten in the state of Denmark. (I.iv,89)

4. Revenge his foul and most unnatural murder. (I.v,24)

5. Taint not thy mind, nor let thy soul contrive
   Against thy mother aught. Leave her to Heaven
   And to those thorns that in her bosom lodge
   To prick and sting her. (I.v,85-88)

6. Though this be madness, yet there is method in't. (II.ii,207)

7. What a piece of work is a man!
   How noble in reason! How infinite in faculty! In form and moving how express and admirable! In action how like an angel! In apprehension how like a god! The beauty of the world! The paragon of animals! And yet, to me, what is this quintessence of dust? Man delights not me -- no, nor woman neither, though by your smiling you seem to say so. (II.ii,315-321)

8. The play's the thing
   Wherein I'll catch the conscience of the King. (II.ii,633-634)

9. The lady doth protest too much, methinks. (III.ii,240)

10. My words fly up, my thoughts remain below.
    Words without thoughts never to Heaven go. (III.iii,97-98)

Hamlet Multiple Choice Unit Test 2 Page 6
Quotations Continued

11. O Hamlet, speak no more.
    Thou turn'st mine eyes into my very soul,
    And there I see such black and grained spots
    As will not leave their tinct. (III.iv,88-91)

12. I must be cruel only to be kind. (III.iv.178)

13.   Oh, from this time forth,
    My thoughts be bloody or be nothing worth. (IV.iv,65-66)

14. Sweets to the sweet. (V.i,266)

15. I am justly killed with mine own treachery. (V.ii,318)

16. The drink, the drink! I am poisoned. (V.ii,321)

17. The King, the King's to blame. (V.ii,331)

Hamlet Multiple Choice Unit Test 2 Page 6

IV. Vocabulary

____	1. PITEOUS	A. Unprincipled
____	2. CONTRIVE	B. To plan with cleverness or ingenuity; scheme
____	3. FILIAL	C. Great happiness; bliss
____	4. FELICITY	D. Immune to attack; impregnable; impossible to damage, injure, or wound
____	5. SCOURGE	E. A means of inflicting severe suffering, vengeance or punishment
____	6. PORTENTOUS	F. Exciting wonder and awe
____	7. CARNAL	G. A model of excellence or perfection
____	8. CONJURATION	H. The relationship of child or offspring to parent
____	9. AMBIGUOUS	I. High praise
____	10. PERDITION	J. Loss of the soul; eternal damnation
____	11. BESEECH	K. Ability or power to decide responsibly
____	12. PERNICIOUS	L. A harmful, corrupting influence
____	13. INVULNERABLE	M. Influence or effect by a supernatural power
____	14. PARAGON	N. Deadly; destructive; wicked
____	15. ALOOF	O. Open to more than one interpretation
____	16. EXTOLMENT	P. Distant physically or emotionally
____	17. CHURLISH	Q. Demanding or arousing pity
____	18. KNAVISH	R. Difficult to work with
____	19. CONTAGION	S. Of or relating to the body or flesh; bodily
____	20. DISCRETION	T. To address an earnest or urgent request to

ANSWER SHEET - *Hamlet*
Multiple Choice Unit Tests

I. Matching	II. Multiple Choice	III. Quotes	IV. Vocabulary
1. ___	1. ___	1. ___	1. ___
2. ___	2. ___	2. ___	2. ___
3. ___	3. ___	3. ___	3. ___
4. ___	4. ___	4. ___	4. ___
5. ___	5. ___	5. ___	5. ___
6. ___	6. ___	6. ___	6. ___
7. ___	7. ___	7. ___	7. ___
8. ___	8. ___	8. ___	8. ___
9. ___	9. ___	9. ___	9. ___
10. ___	10. ___	10. ___	10. ___
11. ___	11. ___	11. ___	11. ___
	12. ___	12. ___	12. ___
	13. ___	13. ___	13. ___
	14. ___	14. ___	14. ___
	15. ___	15. ___	15. ___
	16. ___	16. ___	16. ___
	17. ___	17. ___	17. ___
	18. ___		18. ___
	19. ___		19. ___
			20. ___

ANSWER KEY MULTIPLE CHOICE UNIT TESTS – HAMLET

Answers to Unit Test 1 are in the left column. Answers to Unit Test 2 are in the right column.

I. Matching		II. Multiple Choice		III. Quotes		IV. Vocabulary	
1. D	K	1. D	A	1. A	F	1. E	Q
2. G	I	2. A	C	2. E	G	2. L	B
3. I	G	3. C	B	3. G	E	3. G	H
4. J	A	4. D	B	4. C	D	4. Q	C
5. A	E	5. C	C	5. C	D	5. J	E
6. H	C	6. B	B	6. E	G	6. B	F
7. E	J	7. B	D	7. A	F	7. O	S
8. K	D	8. C	A	8. A	F	8. K	M
9. F	B	9. C	D	9. B	J	9. N	O
10. C	H	10. B	C	10. D	C	10. T	J
11. B	F	11. B	A	11. B	J	11. I	T
		12. B	D	12. A	F	12. M	N
		13. B	D	13. A	F	13. F	D
		14. A	C	14. B	J	14. A	G
		15. D	A	15. F	H	15. R	P
		16. B	B	16. B	J	16. S	I
		17. C	D	17. F	H	17. D	R
		18. D	A			18. C	A
		19. A	C			19. P	L
						20. H	K

UNIT RESOURCE MATERIALS

BULLETIN BOARD IDEAS - *Hamlet*

1. Leave a portion of the bulletin board for the students' best writing assignments.

2. Write out some of the significant quotes from the play on colorful construction paper. Cut out letters to title the board SHAKESPEARE'S *Hamlet*.

3. Take one of the word search puzzles and draw it (enlarged) on the bulletin board. Write the clue words to find to one side. Invite students to take pens and find and circle the words in the time before and after class (or perhaps if they finish their work early).

4. If your library has a picture file, look through it to find people and scenes which look like they could represent characters or scenes from *Hamlet*. Post them on colorful paper on your bulletin board. If your library (school or public) does not have a picture file, try looking in some magazines for pictures.

5. Make a bulletin board posting the crisis hotline numbers for your area and telling what each is for.

6. Post articles of criticism about the play.

7. Make a bulletin board listing the vocabulary words for this unit. As you complete sections of the play and discuss the vocabulary for each section, write the definitions on the bulletin board. (If your board is one students face frequently, it will help them learn the words.)

8. Make a bulletin board about Shakespeare and his works. Put a picture of Shakespeare in the center of your board. Post a little biography of Shakespeare under it. All around it, write the titles of all the plays he wrote or post little "playbills" for each of his plays all around the picture.

9. Have one of your classes do a full production of *Hamlet*. Take pictures and use them for your future bulletin boards. (Your newspaper or yearbook staff would probably be glad to take the pictures for you!)

EXTRA ACTIVITIES

One of the difficulties in teaching literature is that all students don't read at the same speed. One student who likes to read may take the book home and finish it in a day or two. Sometimes a few students finish the in-class assignments early. The problem, then, is finding suitable extra activities for students.

The best thing I've found is to keep a little library in the classroom. For this unit on *Hamlet,* you might check out from the school library other related books and articles about Elizabethan drama, history of the period, court life, etc. Also, you might include other works by Shakespeare (either in original text or simplified versions) and articles of criticism about *Hamlet*.

Other things you may keep on hand are puzzles. I have made some relating directly to *Hamlet* for you. Feel free to duplicate them.

Some students may like to draw. You might devise a contest or allow some extra-credit grade for students who draw characters or scenes from *Hamlet*. Note, too, that if the students do not want to keep their drawings you may pick up some extra bulletin board materials this way. If you have a contest and you supply the prize (a record album or something like that perhaps), you could, possibly, make the drawing itself a non-returnable entry fee.

The pages which follow contain games, puzzles and worksheets. The keys, when appropriate, immediately follow the puzzle or worksheet. There are two main groups of activities: one group for the unit; that is, generally relating to the *Hamlet* text, and another group of activities related strictly to the *Hamlet* vocabulary.

Directions for these games, puzzles and worksheets are self-explanatory. The object here is to provide you with extra materials you may use in any way you choose.

MORE ACTIVITIES - *Hamlet*

1. Have students design a playbill for *Hamlet*.

2. Have students design a bulletin board (ready to be put up; not just sketched) for *Hamlet*.

3. Use some of the related topics (noted earlier for an in-class library) as topics for research, reports or written papers, or as topics for guest speakers.

4. Find a film version of *Hamlet*, show it, and have students evaluate it in comparison to the play.

5. Have students act out the final act of the play on your school's stage. Assign parts. Other students should work together to design the actors' costumes and the set. Lines may or may not be memorized (teacher's decision). Perhaps you could present it to another section or two of English classes during your normal class period. (Provide a background narrative for the audience.)

6. Instead of making a whole production, assign a character to each student. Have that student design his or her own costume, memorize a short passage from the play, and recite the passage (in costume) in front of the class.

7. Have an Elizabethan day in your class. Have students dress up in Elizabethan costume, play music from the period, decorate your room as a castle banquet hall, and have students each bring something for a meal of the time. This will also require some research and planning on the part of the students.

8. Spend a day with a film or slide presentation of castles in England and Scotland.

9. Find someone to give a demonstration of dueling in the times of kings and castles (or to come and speak about the history of dueling).

WORD SEARCH - *Hamlet*

All words in this list are associated with *Hamlet*. The words are placed backwards, forward, diagonally, up and down. The included words are listed below the word searches.

```
H Y T H W G V G E O V E W L J X T K K J J K N S
Y H L X Q W E G G S I S N R T W S A M K Y J R N
P T C M Q Q N R K D K T C G Y Z H J P Z G E R T
V V H T F E S Y T L H H A I L K V T M E G J G H
F E C I V P Z P E R N M R R A K C A G S R L X
F O M E N P L U O A U N B Z O S N I A E A T Y L
Y O R I C K R A M N E D M E T H O D N V D T R T
F U P T T C I O Y T G Y E A E N R F E G E E K Y
G L Q P I L W N T P D E C A B I A G M L J L V G
J H L O E N W E G E N T V P N D S R M E L C U J
E F O H L J B B L O S E Z K O M L A C A N I K X
B N P S P I K R S S N T X K E L H T E N L V K L
W O Y K T H L I A S I D Z E V S O R M D E D L D
F L R M Z F O O T S V N S F U L T N E X X S M L
P V J R C P C E S R L S O I Z E M N I L Y Q O C
F S Y X O S E B Y P B H D R S M S X T U G X M R
D F Q H D W V P D L J U W G E T H T L V S P W F
C X R Y S F E Z D M A D Q C E V D D Q V S P R W
Q B K V X J Z R D L C D T R R K V R Q P B F T M
B Y H V X M N R C X G R N P B H K B T L Q S G T
```

BE	FORTINBRAS	LAERTES	ROSENCRANTZ
BORROWER	GERTRUDE	MAD	SEEMS
CAT	GHOST	METHOD	SOLILOQUY
CLAUDIUS	GRAVE	OPHELIA	SPONGE
CRUEL	GUILDENSTERN	OSRIC	SWEETS
DAGGERS	HAMLET	PLAY	TAPESTRY
DEATH	HEAVEN	POISON	THINKING
DENMARK	HORATIO	POLONIUS	TIME
DRINK	KILLED	PROTEST	WOMAN
ELSINORE	KIN	REJECT	YORICK
ENGLAND	KING	REVENGE	

KEY: WORD SEARCH - *Hamlet*

All words in this list are associated with *Hamlet*. The words are placed backwards, forward, diagonally, up and down. The included words are listed below the word searches.

```
                G       E   O       E               T                       S
                    E   G       I       N               A               R
        T           N   R           T   C   G       H   P           E
            H       E   S   T   L       A   I   L       T   E   G
    F   E       I   V   P       P   E   R   N           R   R   A   K       A   G   S   R
        O   M   E   N   P   L   U   O   A   U       B   Z   O   S   N   I   A   E   A   T
    Y   O   R   I   C   K   R   A   M   N   E   D   M   E   T   H   O   D   N   V   D   T   R
        U       T   T   C   I   O   Y       G       E   A   E   N   R       E   G   E   E       Y
    G       Q       I   L   W   N   T           E   C   A       I   A       M   L   J               G
        H       O   E   N       E   G   E   N       V   P   N       S   R   M   E   L           U
    E       O   H   L       B       L   O   S   E       K   O   M       A   C   A           I
    B       P   S       I       R   S   S   N   T           E   L   H   T   E   N   L       K
        O       T       L   I   A   S   I           E           S   O   R       D   E
            R               O   O   T   S       N   S       U           T   N   E               S
                    R       P       E   S           O   I       E       N   I                       O
                        O       E                   D   R       S           U                   R
                            W               U           E   T                       S
                        S       E       M   A   D           E
                                R       L                   R
                                    C               N
```

BE	FORTINBRAS	LAERTES	ROSENCRANTZ
BORROWER	GERTRUDE	MAD	SEEMS
CAT	GHOST	METHOD	SOLILOQUY
CLAUDIUS	GRAVE	OPHELIA	SPONGE
CRUEL	GUILDENSTERN	OSRIC	SWEETS
DAGGERS	HAMLET	PLAY	TAPESTRY
DEATH	HEAVEN	POISON	THINKING
DENMARK	HORATIO	POLONIUS	TIME
DRINK	KILLED	PROTEST	WOMAN
ELSINORE	KIN	REJECT	YORICK
ENGLAND	KING	REVENGE	

CROSSWORD - *Hamlet*

CROSSWORD CLUES - *Hamlet*

ACROSS
1. Rosencrantz and Guildenstern prepare to take Hamlet there
8. The ___ will mew and the dog will have his day.
9. Hamlet's home
11. A little more than ___ & less than kind
12. Polonius & Laertes tell Ophelia to ___ Hamlet's affections
13. I will speak ____ to her, but use none.
15. Those who tell falsehoods
16. Hamlet wonders whether a miserable life is beter than the unknown of _____
19. The ___, the ___'s to blame.
21. The queen dies after taking the poisoned ___ meant for Hamlet
22. Not difficult
23. Polonius thinks Hamlet has gone ___ because of Ophelia's rejections
26. I must be ____ only to be kind.
27. ____, madam! Nay, it is. I know not ___.
29. The ___ is out of joint.
30. Neither a ___ nor a lender be.
33. Sees his father's ghost and plans to get revenge for his father's murder
34. Descriptive word Hamlet uses for Rosencrantz and Guildenstern
36. The ---- on Laertes' sword kills Hamlet
38. Oh, shame! Where is thy ----?
40. Frailty, thy name is ____!
42. Hamlet runs his sword through it, killing Polonius who was hiding there
44. Elsinore to Hamlet
46. There is nothing either good or bad but ___ makes it so.
47. ____ & Guildenstern

DOWN
2. Hamlet sees the ___ of his father
3. Something is rotten in the state of ____.
4. Tells Hamlet of the wager the King made on Hamlet's behalf
5. Prince of Norway; wants to regain lands his father lost
6. Hamlet's mother
7. Though this be madness, yet there is ___ in't.
8. Hamlet's uncle, the new King
10. Leave her to ___/And to those thorns that in her bosom lodge....
11. Claudius wants Hamlet ___ when he reaches England
14. Hamlet jumps into Ophelia's ___
17. Old schoolmate and friend of Hamlet
18. Polonius' son
20. Rosencrantz and _____
24. To thine own self be ---.
25. The lady doth ____ too much, methinks.
28. Monologue by a character
30. To __ or not to __
31. Laertes wants ___ for his father's death
32. She goes crazy and drowns
35. The ____'s the thing
37. To be or --- to be
39. _____ to the _____
41. Hamlet's mother didn't --- his father's death very long
43. Hamlet ---- and raves pretending to be mad
45. Belonging to us

125

CROSSWORD ANSWER KEY - *Hamlet*

MATCHING QUIZ/WORKSHEET 1 - *Hamlet*

____ 1. OPHELIA   A. She goes crazy and drowns

____ 2. DEATH   B. Sees his father's ghost and plans to get revenge for his father's murder

____ 3. TIME   C. Tells Hamlet of the wager the King made on Hamlet's behalf

____ 4. OSRIC   D. Hamlet jumps into Ophelia's ___

____ 5. DAGGERS   E. Monologue by a character

____ 6. SOLILOQUY   F. The ---- on Laertes' sword kills Hamlet

____ 7. GHOST   G. There is nothing either good or bad but ___ makes it so.

____ 8. KING   H. I will speak ____ to her, but use none.

____ 9. POISON   I. The lady doth ____ too much, methinks.

____ 10. TAPESTRY   J. The ___, the ___'s to blame.

____ 11. DENMARK   K. The ___ will mew and the dog will have his day.

____ 12. THINKING   L. Hamlet runs his sword through it, killing Polonius who was hiding there

____ 13. HAMLET   M. Hamlet sees the ___ of his father

____ 14. LAERTES   N. The ___ is out of joint.

____ 15. GRAVE   O. Hamlet wonders whether a miserable life is beter than the unknown of _____

____ 16. REVENGE   P. Laertes wants ___ for his father's death

____ 17. DRINK   Q. The queen dies after taking the poisoned ___ meant for Hamlet

____ 18. ENGLAND   R. Polonius' son

____ 19. CAT   S. Rosencrantz and Guildenstern prepare to take Hamlet there

____ 20. PROTEST   T. Something is rotten in the state of ____.

KEY: MATCHING QUIZ/WORKSHEET 1 - *Hamlet*

_A_	1. OPHELIA	A. She goes crazy and drowns
_O_	2. DEATH	B. Sees his father's ghost and plans to get revenge for his father's murder
_N_	3. TIME	C. Tells Hamlet of the wager the King made on Hamlet's behalf
_C_	4. OSRIC	D. Hamlet jumps into Ophelia's ___
_H_	5. DAGGERS	E. Monologue by a character
_E_	6. SOLILOQUY	F. The ---- on Laertes' sword kills Hamlet
_M_	7. GHOST	G. There is nothing either good or bad but ___ makes it so.
_J_	8. KING	H. I will speak ____ to her, but use none.
_F_	9. POISON	I. The lady doth ____ too much, methinks.
_L_	10. TAPESTRY	J. The ___, the ___'s to blame.
_T_	11. DENMARK	K. The ___ will mew and the dog will have his day.
_G_	12. THINKING	L. Hamlet runs his sword through it, killing Polonius who was hiding there
_B_	13. HAMLET	M. Hamlet sees the ___ of his father
_R_	14. LAERTES	N. The ___ is out of joint.
_D_	15. GRAVE	O. Hamlet wonders whether a miserable life is better than the unknown of _____
_P_	16. REVENGE	P. Laertes wants ___ for his father's death
_Q_	17. DRINK	Q. The queen dies after taking the poisoned ___ meant for Hamlet
_S_	18. ENGLAND	R. Polonius' son
_K_	19. CAT	S. Rosencrantz and Guildenstern prepare to take Hamlet there
_I_	20. PROTEST	T. Something is rotten in the state of ____.

MATCHING QUIZ/WORKSHEET 2 - *Hamlet*

____ 1. REVENGE   A. Laertes wants ___ for his father's death

____ 2. OSRIC   B. ____ & Guildenstern

____ 3. METHOD   C. Hamlet runs his sword through it, killing Polonius who was hiding there

____ 4. MAD   D. Prince of Norway; wants to regain lands his father lost

____ 5. POLONIUS   E. Hamlet's mother

____ 6. HAMLET   F. Polonius & Laertes tell Ophelia to ___ Hamlet's affections

____ 7. ELSINORE   G. The ___ will mew and the dog will have his day.

____ 8. REJECT   H. Sees his father's ghost and plans to get revenge for his father's murder

____ 9. DRINK   I. Though this be madness, yet there is ___ in't.

____ 10. ROSENCRANTZ   J. _____ to the _____

____ 11. FORTINBRAS   K. Hamlet jumps into Ophelia's ___

____ 12. PROTEST   L. The queen dies after taking the poisoned ___ meant for Hamlet

____ 13. SWEETS   M. Old schoolmate and friend of Hamlet

____ 14. GERTRUDE   N. Something is rotten in the state of ____.

____ 15. LAERTES   O. Ophelia's father

____ 16. TAPESTRY   P. Tells Hamlet of the wager the King made on Hamlet's behalf

____ 17. DENMARK   Q. Polonius thinks Hamlet has gone ___ because of Ophelia's rejections

____ 18. CAT   R. Hamlet's home

____ 19. HORATIO   S. Polonius's son

____ 20. GRAVE   T. The lady doth ____ too much, methinks.

KEY: MATCHING QUIZ/WORKSHEET 2 - *Hamlet*

_A_ 1. REVENGE	A.	Laertes wants ___ for his father's death
_P_ 2. OSRIC	B.	___ & Guildenstern
_I_ 3. METHOD	C.	Hamlet runs his sword through it, killing Polonius who was hiding there
_Q_ 4. MAD	D.	Prince of Norway; wants to regain lands his father lost
_O_ 5. POLONIUS	E.	Hamlet's mother
_H_ 6. HAMLET	F.	Polonius & Laertes tell Ophelia to ___ Hamlet's affections
_R_ 7. ELSINORE	G.	The ___ will mew and the dog will have his day.
_F_ 8. REJECT	H.	Sees his father's ghost and plans to get revenge for his father's murder
_L_ 9. DRINK	I.	Though this be madness, yet there is ___ in't.
_B_ 10. ROSENCRANTZ	J.	_____ to the _____
_D_ 11. FORTINBRAS	K.	Hamlet jumps into Ophelia's ___
_T_ 12. PROTEST	L.	The queen dies after taking the poisoned ___ meant for Hamlet
_J_ 13. SWEETS	M.	Old schoolmate and friend of Hamlet
_E_ 14. GERTRUDE	N.	Something is rotten in the state of ___.
_S_ 15. LAERTES	O.	Ophelia's father
_C_ 16. TAPESTRY	P.	Tells Hamlet of the wager the King made on Hamlet's behalf
_N_ 17. DENMARK	Q.	Polonius thinks Hamlet has gone ___ because of Ophelia's rejections
_G_ 18. CAT	R.	Hamlet's home
_M_ 19. HORATIO	S.	Polonius's son
_K_ 20. GRAVE	T.	The lady doth ___ too much, methinks.

JUGGLE LETTER REVIEW GAME CLUE SHEET - *Hamlet*

SCRAMBLED	WORD	CLUE
EB	BE	To __ or not to __
ROBERWOR	BORROWER	Neither a ___ nor a lender be.
TAC	CAT	The ___ will mew and the dog will have his day.
UDAILSUC	CLAUDIUS	Hamlet's uncle, the new King
LECUR	CRUEL	I must be ____ only to be kind.
GERSAGD	DAGGERS	I will speak ____ to her, but use none.
HEADT	DEATH	Hamlet wonders whether a miserable life is better than the unknown of _____
KADMREN	DENMARK	Something is rotten in the state of ____.
KRIDN	DRINK	The queen dies after taking the poisoned ___ meant for Hamlet
ORSLINEE	ELSINORE	Hamlet's home
DENNLAG	ENGLAND	Rosencrantz and Guildenstern prepare to take Hamlet there
STINRBFARO	FORTINBRAS	Prince of Norway; wants to regain lands his father lost
EUTRDGER	GERTRUDE	Hamlet's mother
SHOTG	GHOST	Hamlet sees the ___ of his father
VAGRE	GRAVE	Hamlet jumps into Ophelia's ___
SNDLGEENRUIT	GUILDENSTERN	Rosencrantz and _____
MATHEL	HAMLET	Sees his father's ghost and plans to get revenge for his father's murder
NAVEHE	HEAVEN	Leave her to ___/And to those thorns that in her bosom lodge....
ORATIOH	HORATIO	Old schoolmate and friend of Hamlet
DELLIK	KILLED	Claudius wants Hamlet ___ when he reaches England
NKI	KIN	A little more than ___ & less than kind
GKNI	KING	The ___, the ___'s to blame.
EESATLR	LAERTES	Polonius' son
DMA	MAD	Polonius thinks Hamlet has gone ___ because of Ophelia's rejections
DOTHEM	METHOD	Though this be madness, yet there is ___ in't.
AIEOHLP	OPHELIA	She goes crazy and drowns
SOCIR	OSRIC	Tells Hamlet of the wager the King made on Hamlet's behalf
YLPA	PLAY	The ____'s the thing
NOISOP	POISON	The ---- on Laertes' sword kills Hamlet
UINLOPSO	POLONIUS	Ophelia's father
STEPROT	PROTEST	The lady doth ____ too much, methinks.

CEETJR	REJECT	Polonius & Laertes tell Ophelia to ___ Hamlet's affections
NEEEVRG	REVENGE	Laertes wants ___ for his father's death
NENROZTRCSA	ROSENCRANTZ	___ & Guildenstern
MEESS	SEEMS	___, madam! Nay, it is. I know not ___.
QLLOOYUIS	SOLILOQUY	Monologue by a character
GONEPS	SPONGE	Descriptive word Hamlet uses for Rosencrantz and Guildenstern
TEESSW	SWEETS	_____ to the _____
PASTYTRE	TAPESTRY	Hamlet runs his sword through it, killing Polonius who was hiding there
GNHNKTII	THINKING	There is nothing either good or bad but ___ makes it so.
MITE	TIME	The ___ is out of joint.
MOWNA	WOMAN	Frailty, thy name is ___!

VOCABULARY RESOURCE MATERIALS

VOCABULARY WORD SEARCH - *Hamlet*

All words in this list are associated with *Hamlet* with an emphasis on the vocabulary words chosen for study in the text. The words are placed backwards, forward, diagonally, up and down. The included words are listed below.

```
J Q T P S U P E R F L U O U S V I S A G E E T R
B W N Z A R R D T A K A P B C U U E I G C A V P
D C G L F R H K N Q R F I G L O O Y G N E J Z T
C Y O E B P A R X C M E Q L U C K E A R E S W W
Z O S M A L A G I D O R P G I N O N T M U W B F
F A N T Y C S F O M Y N I L O F E N A I O O S L
B P I T N N I D F N M B J I I T E L T V P M C C
Y P E M R E W N K L M I T U R C I F S A I G H S
E J O R D I M V V A I E N U R C A U M S G S Q H
S C R R D I V E P U R C P E I A O T H Y I I H Y
D N O S T I S E T C L P T O N I T L I L X Y O H
M I V N Y E T C S A A N U P C T T I R O H K Y N
C G V D V M N I O H B S E I K N P U O C N T D S
P N H U Y O D T O R F A N R E L H S E N I F X N
Q F L L L D C Q O N D R F M A C P E H C N K X K
V N F Z H G M A P U E D L D X B S W I R Q D L Y
D Z Y H F W I M T P S O Y Z M E L L J V P H F X
Q L N C N J R N P I T J Z F B H E E S B Q G X M
D Y T M P W J K G X O C V N D F H L V H P F Y F
C O M M I N G L E D X N N V O W W C H V D B V T
```

ABATEMENTS	CONJURATION	FELICITY	PORTENTOUS
AFFLICT	CONTAGION	FILIAL	PRODIGAL
ALOOF	CONTRIVE	IMMINENT	REPLICATION
AMBIGUOUS	CONVOCATION	INVULNERABLE	SCOURGE
APPURTENANCE	DISCORD	KNAVISH	SINEWS
BASE	DISCRETION	MALICIOUS	SUPERFLUOUS
BESEECH	DIVULGING	PARAGON	VISAGE
CARNAL	ENTREAT	PERDITION	VOW
CHURLISH	EPITAPH	PERNICIOUS	
COMMINGLED	EXTOLMENT	PITEOUS	

KEY: VOCABULARY WORD SEARCH - *Hamlet*

All words in this list are associated with *Hamlet* with an emphasis on the vocabulary words chosen for study in the text. The words are placed backwards, forward, diagonally, up and down. The included words are listed below.

```
            P S U P E R F L U O U S V I S A G E E T
            A       A     A         U U E I   C A
            L   R H   N   R   I       O O   G N E
C   O E   P A R   C   E   L U C K E A R E
  O S   A L A G I D O R P G I N O N T M U W
F A N T   C   F O M   N I L O F E N A I O O S
B P I T N   I   F N M B J I I T E L T V P   C
  P   E   R E   N   L M I T U R C I   S A I   H S
E   O R D I M   V A I E N U R C A U     G S
  C   R D I V E   U R C P E I A O T     I I H
D   O   T I S E T C L P T O N I T   I L     O
  I   N   E T C S A A N U   C T T I R O H   Y N
    V   V   N I O   B S E I   N   U O C N T
      U   O D T O R   A N R E   H   E N I
        L   C   O N D R   M A C   E   C
          G   A   U E   L       B S   I
            I   T P S O         E L L
              N   I T         B   E E
                G X O           F
C O M M I N G L E D     N     V O W
```

ABATEMENTS	CONJURATION	FELICITY	PORTENTOUS
AFFLICT	CONTAGION	FILIAL	PRODIGAL
ALOOF	CONTRIVE	IMMINENT	REPLICATION
AMBIGUOUS	CONVOCATION	INVULNERABLE	SCOURGE
APPURTENANCE	DISCORD	KNAVISH	SINEWS
BASE	DISCRETION	MALICIOUS	SUPERFLUOUS
BESEECH	DIVULGING	PARAGON	VISAGE
CARNAL	ENTREAT	PERDITION	VOW
CHURLISH	EPITAPH	PERNICIOUS	
COMMINGLED	EXTOLMENT	PITEOUS	

VOCABULARY CROSSWORD - *Hamlet*

VOCABULARY CROSSWORD CLUES - *Hamlet*

ACROSS
1. Rashly or wastefully extravagant.
4. Claudius wants Hamlet ___ when he reaches England
5. The ___ will mew and the dog will have his day.
8. The relationship of child or offspring to parent.
9. Open to more than one interpretation.
11. Polonius thinks Hamlet has gone ___ because of Ophelia's rejections
12. To yell out to someone to get their attention
13. Immune to attack; impregnable; impossible to damage, injure, or wound.
16. To ___ or not to ___
17. -- be or not -- be
18. In history; long ago
19. The queen dies after taking the poisoned ___ meant for Hamlet
21. Demanding or arousing pity.
24. Deadly; destructive; wicked.
27. The ___ is out of joint.
28. Singular
29. Becoming known.
31. To make an earnest request of.
37. Full of unspecifiable significance; exciting wonder and awe.
40. Leave her to ___/And to those thorns that in her bosom lodge....
42. ___, madam! Nay, it is. I know not ___.
43. Tension or strife.
44. Descriptive word Hamlet uses for Rosencrantz and Guildenstern
45. Alas, poor _____! I knew him, Horatio.
46. She goes crazy and drowns

DOWN
1. A model of excellence or perfection
2. Ability or power to decide responsibly.
3. To inflict grievous physical or mental suffering on.
4. Unprincipled
5. Difficult to work with.
6. Distant physically or emotionally.
7. A tendon.
10. Spiteful
14. An earnest promise.
15. Something added to another, more important thing; an appendage.
20. The face or facial expression.
22. A means of inflicting severe suffering, vengeance or punishment.
23. Hamlet wonders whether a miserable life is better than the unknown of _____
25. An inscription on a tombstone in memory of the one buried there.
26. Possess
30. To address an earnest or urgent request to.
32. I must be ____ only to be kind.
33. Something is rotten in the state of ____.
34. Old schoolmate and friend of Hamlet
35. Laertes wants ___ for his father's death
36. A little more than ___ & less than kind
38. The ___, the ___'s to blame
39. Hamlet jumps into Ophelia's ___
41. The ____'s the thing

VOCABULARY CROSSWORD ANSWER KEY - *Hamlet*

A filled crossword grid containing the following answers:

Across: PRODIGAL, KILLED, CAT, FILIAL, AMBIGUOUS, MAD, CALL, INVULNERABLE, PAST, DRINK, PITEOUS, PERNICIOUS, TIME, ONE, DIVULGING, ENTREAT, PORTENTOUS, HEAVEN, SEEMS, DISCORD, SPONGE, YORICK, OPHELIA

Down: PARAGON, ARRAS, DISPATCH, IF, CALLOW, AN, FAN, LOVE, SO, ALAS, SHORE, INVULNERABLE, BECKON, DRINK, OVERCAME, FISH, SHOWS, VICIOUS, OBSCURE, USURP, ONE, PIPING, PAST, HURDY, TIME, MEAT, PLAY

VOCABULARY WORSHEET 1 - *Hamlet*

____ 1. Great happiness; bliss
    A. imminent   B. contagion   C. paragon   D. felicity

____ 2. Unprincipled
    A. aloof   B. malicious   C. ambiguous   D. knavish

____ 3. Spiteful
    A. invulnerable   B. discretion   C. commingled   D. malicious

____ 4. To inflict grievous physical or mental suffering on
    A. abatements   B. afflict   C. felicity   D. carnal

____ 5. Rashly or wastefully extravagant
    A. knavish   B. churlish   C. prodigal   D. epitaph

____ 6. Distant physically or emotionally
    A. aloof   B. discord   C. ambiguous   D. filial

____ 7. The relationship of child or offspring to parent
    A. entreat   B. filial   C. appurtenance   D. discord

____ 8. Full of unspecifiable significance; exciting wonder and awe
    A. portentous   B. filial   C. base   D. prodigal

____ 9. To address an earnest or urgent request to
    A. entreat   B. beseech   C. abatements   D. contrive

____ 10. Tendons; muscles
    A. appurtenance   B. invulnerable   C. visage   D. sinews

____ 11. To plan with cleverness or ingenuity; scheme
    A. paragon   B. contrive   C. superfluous   D. filial

____ 12. A means of inflicting severe suffering, vengeance or punishment
    A. prodigal   B. vow   C. scourge   D. carnal

____ 13. The lowest or bottom part
    A. base   B. beseech   C. contrive   D. epitaph

____ 14. A harmful, corrupting influence
    A. malicious   B. filial   C. entreat   D. contagion

____ 15. About to occur; impending
    A. imminent   B. discretion   C. discord   D. pernicious

____ 16. An inscription on a tombstone in memory of the one buried there
    A. perdition   B. discord   C. vow   D. epitaph

____ 17. Reduction in amount, degree, or intensity
    A. entreat   B. contagion   C. divulging   D. abatements

____ 18. The face or facial expression
    A. contagion   B. commingled   C. contrive   D. visage

____ 19. Of or relating to the body or flesh; bodily
    A. malicious   B. imminent   C. prodigal   D. carnal

____ 20. An earnest promise
    A. abatements   B. vow   C. malicious   D. contagion

KEY: VOCABULARY WORKSHEET 1 - *Hamlet*

__D_ 1. Great happiness; bliss
    A. imminent   B. contagion   C. paragon   D. felicity

__D_ 2. Unprincipled
    A. aloof   B. malicious   C. ambiguous   D. knavish

__D_ 3. Spiteful
    A. invulnerable   B. discretion   C. commingled   D. malicious

__B_ 4. To inflict grievous physical or mental suffering on
    A. abatements   B. afflict   C. felicity   D. carnal

__C_ 5. Rashly or wastefully extravagant
    A. knavish   B. churlish   C. prodigal   D. epitaph

__A_ 6. Distant physically or emotionally
    A. aloof   B. discord   C. ambiguous   D. filial

__B_ 7. The relationship of child or offspring to parent
    A. entreat   B. filial   C. appurtenance   D. discord

__A_ 8. Full of unspecifiable significance; exciting wonder and awe
    A. portentous   B. filial   C. base   D. prodigal

__B_ 9. To address an earnest or urgent request to
    A. entreat   B. beseech   C. abatements   D. contrive

__D_ 10. Tendons; muscles
    A. appurtenance   B. invulnerable   C. visage   D. sinews

__B_ 11. To plan with cleverness or ingenuity; scheme
    A. paragon   B. contrive   C. superfluous   D. filial

__C_ 12. A means of inflicting severe suffering, vengeance or punishment
    A. prodigal   B. vow   C. scourge   D. carnal

__A_ 13. The lowest or bottom part
    A. base   B. beseech   C. contrive   D. epitaph

__D_ 14. A harmful, corrupting influence
    A. malicious   B. filial   C. entreat   D. contagion

__A_ 15. About to occur; impending
    A. imminent   B. discretion   C. discord   D. pernicious

__D_ 16. An inscription on a tombstone in memory of the one buried there
    A. perdition   B. discord   C. vow   D. epitaph

__D_ 17. Reduction in amount, degree, or intensity
    A. entreat   B. contagion   C. divulging   D. abatements

__D_ 18. The face or facial expression
    A. contagion   B. commingled   C. contrive   D. visage

__D_ 19. Of or relating to the body or flesh; bodily
    A. malicious   B. imminent   C. prodigal   D. carnal

__B_ 20. An earnest promise
    A. abatements   B. vow   C. malicious   D. contagion

VOCABULARY WORKSHEET 2 - *Hamlet*

____ 1. EXTOLMENT   A. Influence or effect by a supernatural power

____ 2. PORTENTOUS   B. Tension or strife

____ 3. CONJURATION   C. The face or facial expression

____ 4. PRODIGAL   D. Ability or power to decide responsibly

____ 5. REPLICATION   E. The lowest or bottom part

____ 6. CARNAL   F. Unprincipled

____ 7. PARAGON   G. Demanding or arousing pity

____ 8. DISCORD   H. Of or relating to the body or flesh; bodily

____ 9. ENTREAT   I. To make an earnest request of

____ 10. PERDITION   J. Immune to attack; impregnable; impossible to damage, injure, or wound

____ 11. BASE   K. Distant physically or emotionally

____ 12. EPITAPH   L. Exciting wonder and awe

____ 13. ALOOF   M. Being beyond what is required or sufficient

____ 14. PITEOUS   N. High praise

____ 15. INVULNERABLE   O. A reply to an answer; a rejoinder

____ 16. SUPERFLUOUS   P. Loss of the soul; eternal damnation

____ 17. KNAVISH   Q. An inscription on a tombstone in memory of the one buried there

____ 18. DISCRETION   R. A model of excellence or perfection

____ 19. DIVULGING   S. Rashly or wastefully extravagant

____ 20. VISAGE   T. Becoming known

KEY: VOCABULARY WORKSHEET 2 - *Hamlet*

_N_	1. EXTOLMENT	A. Influence or effect by a supernatural power
_L_	2. PORTENTOUS	B. Tension or strife
_A_	3. CONJURATION	C. The face or facial expression
_S_	4. PRODIGAL	D. Ability or power to decide responsibly
_O_	5. REPLICATION	E. The lowest or bottom part
_H_	6. CARNAL	F. Unprincipled
_R_	7. PARAGON	G. Demanding or arousing pity
_B_	8. DISCORD	H. Of or relating to the body or flesh; bodily
_I_	9. ENTREAT	I. To make an earnest request of
_P_	10. PERDITION	J. Immune to attack; impregnable; impossible to damage, injure, or wound
_E_	11. BASE	K. Distant physically or emotionally
_Q_	12. EPITAPH	L. Exciting wonder and awe
_K_	13. ALOOF	M. Being beyond what is required or sufficient
_G_	14. PITEOUS	N. High praise
_J_	15. INVULNERABLE	O. A reply to an answer; a rejoinder
_M_	16. SUPERFLUOUS	P. Loss of the soul; eternal damnation
_F_	17. KNAVISH	Q. An inscription on a tombstone in memory of the one buried there
_D_	18. DISCRETION	R. A model of excellence or perfection
_T_	19. DIVULGING	S. Rashly or wastefully extravagant
_C_	20. VISAGE	T. Becoming known

VOCABULARY JUGGLE LETTER REVIEW GAME CLUES - *Hamlet*

SCRAMBLED	WORD	CLUE
STORPOEUNT	PORTENTOUS	Full of unspecifiable significance; exciting wonder and awe
RNNEALBEULVI	INVULNERABLE	Immune to attack; impregnable; impossible to damage, injure, or wound
CIASULOMI	MALICIOUS	Spiteful
LAFLII	FILIAL	The relationship of child or offspring to parent
DLGAORPI	PRODIGAL	Rashly or wastefully extravagant
VWO	VOW	An earnest promise
NSOPCIREUI	PERNICIOUS	Deadly; destructive; wicked
BSUUIAMOG	AMBIGUOUS	Open to more than one interpretation
LFACTIF	AFFLICT	To inflict grievous physical or mental suffering on
CNIOERDTSI	DISCRETION	Ability or power to decide responsibly
TTRENAE	ENTREAT	To make an earnest request of
HECESBE	BESEECH	To address an earnest or urgent request to
NRIEVTCO	CONTRIVE	To plan with cleverness or ingenuity; scheme
RONAPGA	PARAGON	A model of excellence or perfection of a king
PRNECAUPETNA	APPURTENANCE	Something added to another, more important thing; an appendage
PTPAHIE	EPITAPH	An inscription on a tombstone in memory of the one buried there
MGDENOLMCI	COMMINGLED	Mixed together
VHKANIS	KNAVISH	Unprincipled
TNOAGINOC	CONTAGION	A harmful, corrupting influence
WISSNE	SINEWS	Tendons; muscles
SEAGIV	VISAGE	The face or facial expression
SETUIPO	PITEOUS	Demanding or arousing pity
ORESGUC	SCOURGE	A means of inflicting severe suffering, vengeance or punishment
LGNDIUGIV	DIVULGING	Becoming known
RSOCDID	DISCORD	Tension or strife
PTONILRACEI	REPLICATION	A reply to an answer; a rejoinder
VAONONCOTIC	CONVOCATION	Assembly
METNINIM	IMMINENT	About to occur; impending
LRUFOSUPEUS	SUPERFLUOUS	Being beyond what is required or sufficient

Hamlet Vocabulary Juggle Letter Review Game Continued

NSABEMETTA	ABATEMENTS	Reduction in amount, degree, or intensity
SAEB	BASE	The lowest or bottom part
RCUSHHIL	CHURLISH	Difficult to work with
RUJNIOCNTAO	CONJURATION	Influence or effect by a supernatural power
TRNOPDIIE	PERDITION	Loss of the soul; eternal damnation
LEXOENTMT	EXTOLMENT	High praise
OFALO	ALOOF	Distant physically or emotionally
ITYCFLEI	FELICITY	Great happiness; bliss
RALNAC	CARNAL	Of or relating to the body or flesh; bodily

www.ingramcontent.com/pod-product-compliance
Lightning Source LLC
Chambersburg PA
CBHW051413070526
44584CB00023B/3404